Off (
Festival Plays

33rd Series

Selected by New York theatre critics, professionals, and the editorial
staff of Samuel French, Inc. as the most important plays of the
33rd Off Off Broadway Original Short Play Festival.

F*CKING ART
by Bekah Brunstetter

AYRAVANA FLIES or A PRETTY DISH
by Sheila Callaghan

THE THREAD MEN
by Thomas C. Dunn

THE DYING BREED
by Thomas Higgins

THE GRAVE
by Gabe McKinley

JUNIPER; JUBILEE
by Janine Nabers

SAMUEL FRENCH

FOUNDED 1830

NEW YORK HOLLYWOOD LONDON TORONTO

SAMUELFRENCH.COM

IMPORTANT BILLING AND CREDIT
REQUIREMENTS

Dear Friend,

I am pleased to introduce you to the winners of the **33rd Annual Samuel French Off Off Broadway Short Play Festival**. We are very happy to share these exciting and inventive new plays with you.

Our 33rd year marked a turning point in the festival's long history. We settled into a new venue, the Peter Jay Sharp Theater, for the festivities. We put in place an accelerated timeline for the event, increasing the pace and ratcheting up the festival spirit. We also made an effort to increase the visibility of the festival, in order to make it a more valuable experience for all of the playwrights and producing companies involved. With the 33rd festival, and as we move forward toward future festivals, we aim to make the experience a useful and pleasant one for all concerned.

To that end, on a more personal note, I would like to extend my congratulations to all the playwrights who were featured in the 33rd festival, and thank the producing companies for their hard work and dedication to new plays. It is heartening to find such a wealth of talent, and I am proud that we at Samuel French are introducing it to a wider audience. In addition, I would like to thank the agents and playwrights who volunteered their time to act as judges. Their commitment to the craft of playwriting is admirable, and their support vital to the success of this festival.

This festival has been a stepping stone to greater success for many now established playwrights. It is my hope that the reach of the festival will continue to grow and provide opportunities for early-career playwrights for years to come. Such a strong showcase and opportunity for development is vital to the maintenance of a healthy and vibrant theatrical community. I feel it is both the company's responsibility and my personal pleasure to help foster new work into existence.

Please enjoy the 33rd Series of the Off-Off Broadway Festival Plays!

Sincerely,

Leon Embry
President and C.E.O.
Samuel French, Inc.

33RD ANNUAL SAMUEL FRENCH OFF OFF BROADWAY SHORT PLAY FESTIVAL JULY 15TH – 20TH PETER JAY SHARP THEATER NYC

SAMUEL FRENCH

OOB

FESTIVAL

The Samuel French Off-Off Broadway festival started in 1975 and is Manhattan's oldest continuous short play festival. Hundreds of theatre companies and schools have participated in the Festival's first thirty-three years, including companies from coast to coast as well as abroad from Canada and England. This festival has served as a doorway to future success for many aspiring writers. Over the years, 181 submitted plays have been published, and many of the participants have become established, award-winning playwrights. The unique aspect of requiring authors to collaborate with a producing organization and present their work in performance, we hope, encourages the collaborative and creative process of playwriting.

Festival Coordinator: Ken Dingledine
Production Coordinator: Billie Davis
Literary Coordinator: Roxane Heinze-Bradshaw
Assistant Literary Coordinator: Amy Rose Marsh
Press/Public Relations: Cromarty & Company
Layout/Graphic Design: Ryan Hugh McWilliams
Judge Liaison: Emma Halpern
Webmaster: Phillip DeVita
Lighting Design: Miriam Crowe
Board Operator: Syche Hamilton
Festival Crew: Sara Mirowski, Jason Surratt, Brad Lohrenz, Laura Lindson, Lauren Joseph, Kelly Dobitz, Melody Fernandez

SAMUEL FRENCH STAFF JUDGES

Ken Dingledine, **Publications Manager**
Roxane Heinze-Bradshaw, **Managing Editor**
Brad Lohrenz, **Director of Licensing**
Amy Rose Marsh, **Editorial Assistant**
Ryan Hugh McWilliams, **Production Assistant**
Lysna Marzani, **Contracts Manager**
Abbie Van Nostrand, **Vice-President**

Samuel French President & C.E.O.: Leon Embry
Samuel French Vice-President: Abbie Van Nostrand

GUEST JUDGES

Beth Blickers
Thomas Bradshaw
Kathleen Clark
Seth Glewen
Israel Horovitz
Shirley Lauro

Eduardo Machado
Patricia McLaughlin
Jane Milmore
Elsa Neuwald
Mark Orsini
Buddy Thomas

FUCKING ART

by Bekah Brunstetter

For both e. gleckler's

ABOUT THE PRODUCTION

The 33rd Annual Samuel French Off Off Broadway Short Play Festival production of this play included the following people:

ART . . . . Brandon Uranowitz
GAL . . . . Emily Perkins

Director: Stephen Brackett
Produced by: Working Man's Clothes Productions

ABOUT THE AUTHOR

Bekah Brunstetter received her MFA in Playwriting from the New School for Drama. This is her third year with the festival. She is a proud member of the Ars Nova Play Group, and serves as Director of New Play Development for Working Man's Clothes Productions.

(A clean room.

Skinny **ART** *wears comfy clothes and sits on the edge of a white bed with a table next to it.*

Optimistically, he builds a tower of white paper cups.

GAL *stands against the door, petrified, paralyzed. She is that hot girl from high school.*

They are both 18.

Classical music plays, the kind that makes Children go to Sleep.)

ART. So um, are we gonna do this or what?

GAL. No, yeah. We are.

ART. Right Now?

GAL. In a minute. (*hearing music*) What is this, is this like, a hymn?

ART. It's classical music. It's supposed to put you to sleep, especially if you're a little kid. In case you're not the kinda parent who puts brandy in bottles.

GAL. Are you tired?

ART. No.

GAL. It's midnight.

ART. I don't get tired at night anymore.

GAL. Fevers?

ART. Yeah.

(looking at her)

Are you gonna puke?

GAL. No.

ART. Are you scared?

GAL. Just a little freaked out.

ART. Yeah, why?

GAL. Um, the drive. I drove all night and it rained and I got lost. I thought I might slide off the road into a ravine and a raccoon might eat my face and people with face scars make me sad. Um, also, my stomach feels, I ate at a gas station. The bathroom had puke in it, I peed in a bush. My mom thinks I'm sleeping over at my friend Sarah's watching all of the Godfather's. Lying is hard.

ART. (*smiling*) I bet you're good at it.

GAL. I am, it's kinda sad. It's cause I'm an actor, I think.

ART. You're an actor now, huh?

GAL. Yeah, I don't know. I think I wanna be one, or something. No, I like *know* I do.

ART. (*smiling, to himself*) 'The past is the present, isn't it? It's the future too.'

(*pause*)

GAL. What?

ART. Long Day's Journey. (*Pause. She looks blank.*) Into Night.

GAL. Oh, yeah. We haven't gotten that far yet. I'm taking drama this quarter, we're doing monologues. We're still doing Steel Magnolias. And like, Shakespeare.

ART. 'The play's the thing!'

GAL. Shakespeare. Duh. I get it, okay? You know everything.

ART. So you're an actor.

(*She nods distantly.*)

GAL. I mean I like cheerleading and stuff but I don't really see any future in it. Last week Ms. Moriarty made us all bring in mix tapes of songs that were important to us, that like, reflected us, and we had to sit on a stool in front of the whole class while we all listened to it, while it like, moved from song to song. Like three gay kids secretly outted themselves and cried. I didn't cry, though, when it was my turn. I guess I wanted to.

ART. What were your songs?

GAL. Nah, no, I don't wanna tell you.

ART. Why not?

GAL. Cause you have like, untouchable taste, I bet. You listen to like, music made by people who live under rocks in the middle of nowhere. Who like have invented new sounds that come out grass and kitchen appliances. You'd laugh at me, they were all, mine were like, predictable.

ART. (*smiling wryly*) Jewel?

GAL. Shut up.

ART. (*singing*) "Do you hate them – cause they're pieces of you –"

GAL. You don't know me.

ART. Take off your pants.

GAL. What?

ART. Nothing.

(*Pause. She looks at him.*)

GAL. Oh my god, You look like death, Art, you really do, you're so skinny.

ART. I've always been skinny. I coulda been a model.

GAL. No your face, your skin, you're like – not there.

ART. No, actually, I'm here.

GAL. I kinda want to cry, look at you.

(*She puts her hand to her mouth. Pause.*)

Nevermind, I won't. Almost.

(*Pause. The room hums.*)

The room, this whole place, um, I've never been anywhere like it before.

ART. That's a good thing.

GAL. I guess, I guess it's good.

ART. Wait, how would it not be good?

GAL. I don't know, I don't really have anything to say ever. Cause, um, cause nothing ever happens to me ever. Nothing bad ever. I nightmare about hurricanes and food coming to life and those are my only tragedies. My grandmother was part Jewish and I end up talking a lot about this, too, like I was in the fucking Holocaust, like I know how that felt. I correct people when they spell dreidel wrong.

ART. Maybe that's why you like plays.

GAL. What?

ART. People like to borrow other people's tragedies.

GAL. Yeah, I guess I do that.

ART. I bet I would eventually like that about you. If we were to ever, if we became better acquainted.

GAL. I'm not deep like you.

ART. You want to be, I think.

GAL. That doesn't count.

ART. It's better than nothing.

GAL. I missed the game tonight, tonight was a game night, I came here instead.

There might not have been a pyramid at all.

I'm some sort of base, I'm important.

(pause)

ART. ...Thank you?

GAL. No, I didn't mean it like, I didn't say that to make you feel bad.

ART. Come'ere.

GAL. I'm scared to smell you.

ART. Why?

GAL. I'm scared you'll smell like death.

ART. I don't, I smell like a person, I smell like soap.

(Slowly, she moves away from the door. She approaches him. She sits next to him on the bed, gingerly. They sit next to each other.)

I heard you tried to kill yourself cause you didn't get into Julliard.

GAL. I really wanted to go.

ART. It's not even a real college.

GAL. I was planning on going, I was so sure, I just, it just screwed me all up. When I got rejected, when I, I was just so *sure.* I told people I was going.

(Pause. Then quickly:)

I didn't really, um, I didn't really try to kill myself. I just um, there was a rumor that, I missed school and, I let people believe it.

ART. *(smiling)* I know. You wouldn't, you couldn't.

GAL. I fucking could.

ART. No, you *like* life. You obviously like life.

GAL. Yeah, I guess.

(She studies him.)

Can I, um – I kind of want to –

ART. What?

(She takes a manicured hand and places it gently on his neck. He is still.)

GAL. *(quietly)* I just wanted to touch them. Your 'lymph' nodes.

ART. I know what they are.

GAL. That's where the – that's where it is.

ART. I know that, too.

GAL. I know. I just – I want you to know. I – I studied. I retained information, so. Tried to.

ART. So are we / going to –

GAL. Do you want to?

ART. I thought that's why you came.

GAL. No, yeah, I / mean –

ART. 'Dear Art, I want to be your first and last.'

GAL. God, I didn't say it like *that.*

(pause)

Would I – I don't want to like – hurt you.

ART. Ha.

GAL. What?

ART. Too late.

GAL. I just got here, I haven't hurt you yet.

ART. No, sixth grade.

GAL. *F* sixth grade.

ART. Was nothing to you, I guess.

GAL. What?

ART. How much I loved you then.

GAL. No you didn't.

ART. I got over it.

GAL. You didn't *love* me. You recognized the fact that I had boobs or something, congratulations, you and everyone else, get in line. (*pause*) I mean, um. God, I'm a bitch. I don't mean to be such a bitch all the time.

ART. No, I definitely loved you. You were so – weird.

GAL. I – I'm still weird.

ART. And I liked how you treated that rabbit.

GAL. (*smiling*) Oh my god, that fucking rabbit.

ART. Remember when we found her in the parking lot after soccer? Half-maimed by somebody's mommy's mini-van?

GAL. Yeah and Ms. B said we weren't allowed to have a class pet so I hid her in my cubby for 3 whole days. God, I was such a freak.

ART. (*smiling*) Totally inappropriate, inhumane.

GAL. She coulda been hit by a car, she coulda died! I *saved* her.

ART. She *did* die. After three days. You tried, though, good for you. I helped you bury her in a box. It was Easter and I made Cryptic Easter references about the bunny emerging and living for 30 more days.

GAL. Oh. Right. That sucked, I was sad.

ART. It was just her time.

   (*pause*)

GAL. Don't talk like that.

ART. What?

GAL. *It was her time.*

ART. Yeah, It was totally normal for you to keep a rabbit in your cubby like a hippie freak, like a secret soft soul, but I start reading my Bible at lunch and I get my ass beat.

GAL. You shoulda been more careful, you ruined yourself. You coulda kept it to yourself.

ART. ...I *ruined* myself?

GAL. You know, like, thereafter, you became known as the God Kid. The straight edge with no, like, edge.

ART. Oh.

GAL. You coulda kept it to yourself, that's all I'm saying.

ART. That's not the point. Someone tells you the secret of to how to live forever, you don't tell anyone else, you keep it to yourself? No.

GAL. Maybe some people just want to die and have that be that.

ART. No one wants to die.

GAL. Do you ?

(*pause*)

ART. It's not a matter of whether or not I want to at this point, because I'm going to soon, so, preferences dissipate.

(*pause*)

GAL. Right, yeah.

(*pause*)

Stephanie Holiday got into Julliard. Remember her? Yeah, she got in. She's a orphan. Yeah, she was raised by her lesbian aunt whose partner died of girl AIDS. She's totally deep.

(**ART** *resumes building his cup tower. It's getting super awesome high.*)

What are you doing?

ART. Seducing you.

GAL. No you're *not.*

ART. Apparently all I have to do is just sit here and be sick.

GAL. That is *so* not true –

ART. Yes it is.

(*pause*)

ART. What'd you come here for really?

GAL. You said – I mean, I thought – I imagined you being very lonely. Here. Bored.

ART. (*quick*) Not bored at all. They take us on field trips. We go to Walmart, we go shopping, we peruse hand towels and microwaves we'll never need. We see movies, we hang out.

GAL. We?

ART. Me and all the other kids, the nurses.

GAL. In big groups like that?

ART. Yeah.

GAL. That's weird.

ART. And my mom and dad are usually here.

GAL. My mom and dad make me lonely.

ART. Mine don't.

GAL. Where are they?

ART. Youth Pastor convention. I told them to go, I said I needed some me time.

GAL. Are they – are they sad?

ART. Um –

GAL. I've been trying to wonder how sad that feels.

ART. They have peace.

GAL. Really?

ART. Yeah.

GAL. Cause of – God – stuff?

ART. Yeah – God. Stuff.

GAL. Oh.

ART. Because believers belong in heaven so it's like going

Home and whatever you want on the table is there.
You like hot homemade mac and cheese with sausage
chunks and burnty cheese exterior and a big glass of
milk? Done. You want wood floors cause the wood
floors when you were a kid were wood and it was fun
to slide on it in your dirty socks? Done. Wood it is.
You like Woody Guthrie? Done. Every album ever, a
turn table.
Your life tucked into your mansion, every cranny filled
with your favorites.

GAL. What if you wanted a cigarette?

ART. You wouldn't.

GAL. What if you wanted to call someone a motherfucker?

ART. No one would be.

GAL. And who would you be without your body?

*(Pause. ART gets up, slowly, pained, and reaches for his
Bible. GAL looks weary. ART puts it back. He sits down
next to her.)*

ART. Cause like – if you're good, or if you try to be, then
you're rewarded, even if it doesn't seem like a prize at
the time, it turns out that way. Cause God is good.

GAL. I wish I was good.

ART. That's a start.

GAL. I, um – Art?

ART. Uh huh?

GAL. Hi.

ART. Hi.

*(Gingerly, she puts her finger to his hair, then her whole
hand. Slowly, she tossles his hair. She rubs his head. He
closes his eyes. He likes this.)*

Mmm. I like that.

GAL. *(quietly)* You do?

ART. Yeah, my mom does that.

GAL. My sister says boys are only ever trying to have sex
with their moms. *(pause)* I dreamt the other night I

died, I was falling, it was the simplest dream.

(**GAL** *sniffs.*)

Hey, Art?

(Pause. She cannot get this out. Her hands stop moving.)

I um, I looked up all the, all the symptoms, and um, I swear to God, sorry, I mean, I swear to – to someone super important that my – on my neck – it's all swollen, and sometimes I can't sleep, and sometimes my head hurts, and I'm really scared / to –

(**ART** *pulls away. He clears his throat.*)

ART. Wow. You don't have cancer.

GAL. Why not? *You* have cancer.

(**ART** *gets to his feet. He moves back to his tower. This takes a minute.*)

Where are you going?

ART. Socks. For my feet. They're cold.

GAL. Oh.

(**ART** *whips the warm socks his mom bought in fat bags onto his feet. They are so fat, they dwarf him.*)

ART. (*hot*) So you're here to entertain me?

GAL. I – I –

ART. Did you bring UNO? Pocket Scrabble? Should we mod-podge something?

GAL. I know you're pissed, I know you're angry at – I mean, you've got to be so fucking pissed, how UNFAIR all of this, I mean -

It's not fair of you to make me feel bad just because you can.

ART. Yes it is, because guess what, you're kind of a bitch, you've always been a bitch, and now all of the sudden, all of the sudden, I get sick and then I get sent away and then I get two months to live and then ALL OF THE SUDDEN –

(As hard as he can, he whips open the drawer of a bed side table. It falls to the ground. It's filled with letters. He breathes hard, weak. He sits on the bed.)

Yeah.

GAL. I, um. I didn't write you all those.

ART. Yeah, I know. Everyone else did.

GAL. (*quietly*) Who?

ART. Girls, mostly. Girls from fifth grade, girls from tenth grade, bitch girls, popular girls, girls who never looked at me before, girls who looked and me and laughed, girls who looked at me and puked.

And um, friends of my mom's, and stuff.

(*He looks at the pile. He finds a letter. He pulls it out.*)

Stephanie Holiday.

(*He looks at* GAL.)

You thought you were the only one?

GAL. I – I don't know – Yeah, I guess –

ART. I mean – the only one to like *drive* six hours to and put their money where their mouth is, as it were, yeah, but in terms of flowery correspondence, man, get in line.

GAL. What, um. What do they say?

(ART *kneels down about begins placing the letters back into the drawer.*

ART. "Been thinking about you."

"I dreamt we kissed."

"I dreamt you died."

"I always wished that I could say something to you, when I saw you in the halls, but I was too scared, I'm sorry."

"Remember when you came to my house in fifth grade?"

"Weren't you my boyfriend for a minute when we were little?"

"I think you are so brave."

"I'm praying for you."

GAL. Who's praying for you?

ART. Um, you. You said you were praying for me.

GAL. I said that?

ART. Yeah.

GAL. Oh.

(**ART** *replaces the drawer.*)

I meant it, I think. It's kinda messed up to just pray when you want things, or when you're scared/ but...

ART. ACTS. Adoration, Confession / Thanksgiving Supplication.

GAL. Thanksgiving Supplication. I remember, okay? The asking is supposed to come last.

(*Pause.* **ART** *returns to his tower.*)

It's impressive. I mean, um, you – impress me. How you – stuck with – how it – stuck with you. God, and stuff. You're pretty serious about it, huh? I mean, um. Him.

ART. Yeah, we're like totally dating.

GAL. Are you mad at me?

ART. Um, I don't even know you. I could only be mad at you like, in theory. And I'm not.

GAL. Cause you're too good to be mad at people for like, selfish reasons? Cause you / believe in –

ART. Cause I don't sweat the small stuff.

GAL. I'm small stuff?

ART. I barely know you.

GAL. But you could.

ART. What, you mean if I had sex with you?

GAL. No, I mean – *pause.* Are you a virgin?

ART. Oh, okay. Aha.

GAL. No, are you?

(*pause*)

ART. Define virgin.

GAL. Um –

ART. It doesn't matter, why does it matter?

GAL. I don't know, it just / it just –

ART. So okay, so I'm going to take off my pants, okay? Great. And then you're going to slip down to your lace Teddy. I'll put on some Coldplay and you can backwards cowgirl do me back to life.

(pause)

GAL. No.

ART. No?

GAL. That's not how / I –

ART. Ever think that I might have other things on my mind than boning some girl?

GAL. *(quietly)* Yeah – yeah, I know.

ART. So – yeah.

(He returns to his tower.)

GAL. So you don't want to?

ART. *(not looking at her, embarrassed)* Well, I'm human and stuff, and you are hot. And stuff.

GAL. Didn't you make some – um – some pact to like – wait, though?

ART. Yeah, that was always the plan.

GAL. Yeah, I thought so too, I thought you mighta done that.

ART. And yet, here you are. Are you wearing special underwear things?

GAL. I just thought, maybe, like – tragedy suspends rules. I guess that's what I was thinking. Like if there's a flood or a hurricane or the apocalypse and you're suddenly allowed to steal stereos.

ART. It's crossed my mind.

GAL. Are you glad that I'm here?

ART. *(quietly)* Yeah.

GAL. You're gonna die.

ART. I know.

GAL. This time next year, you won't be here anymore.

ART. I know.

(She grabs him, hugs him.)

...OW....

(**GAL** *pulls away.*)

GAL. Oh – Oh my God – did I hurt you – I'm so sorry, I – are you okay?

ART. No, you just pulled my hair. Coulda happened to anybody. Had nothing to do with my eminent death.

(She smooths his hair down. She has no idea how to touch him.)

GAL. Can I give you a gentle hug?

ART. Yeah, okay.

(**GAL** *gathers him her arms, gingerly, then tenderly.*)

GAL. I like this music. It makes me feel grown-up.

ART. Me too.

GAL. Hey, Art?

ART. Yup.

GAL. I wanna tell you something fucked up.

ART. You shouldn't cuss so much. You use your brain more if you don't just revert to profanity.

GAL. It's just my vocabulary.

ART. Try 'truly twisted.'

GAL. I – I want to tell you something – truly – twisted.

ART. Nice.

GAL. But it's fucked up.

ART. Shoot.

(pause)

GAL. I was taking this creative writing class freshmen year and we all had to write poems and I didn't have anything to write about, so I fu – had sex with this guy up the street.

ART. Then what?

GAL. I wrote a poem about it.

ART. And – times thereafter?

GAL. Content.

ART. Still writing poems?

GAL. No.

> *(Pause. The song might turn sad here, or end completely. She is near tears.)*

I wanna be good.

ART. You are good. You came to see me. You missed a game.

GAL. No I wanna be GOOD good, like in my core good.

ART. Maybe you are.

GAL. I'm not, I'm not!

ART. Maybe.

> *(pause)*

GAL. What does God say about empty people? Empty fucking people?

ART. He pretty much loves everyone all the time.

GAL. Like Santa? Like your Mom and Dad?

ART. Like – God.

GAL. What does he do to selfish people?

ART. He loves them.

GAL. Like puppies?

ART. Like his kids.

GAL. Oh.

> *(She looks at him. He looks a little off.)*

GAL. How are you?

ART. Me? I'm great.

GAL. Really?

ART. Really, yeah.

> *(Pause. She gets a wet rag from the bedside table. She dabs it to his forehead.)*

GAL. *(softly)* That feel good?

ART. Yeah, really good.

GAL. Good.

ART. I guess you're not gonna blow me, huh?

> **(GAL** *smiles, laughs.*
>
> **ART** *takes a cup. He puts in on top of the tower. They watch it.)*

GAL. If this were a metaphor, if we were a metaphor, that whole thing would fall over right now.

ART. Yeah.

> *(Pause. They watch it.)*

GAL. What if I said – what if I were to suddenly / say – to Him -

ART. He'd listen.

GAL. Oh. *(pause)* Anytime?

ART. Yeah. It's pretty fucking fantastic actually.

> **(GAL** *smiles. She looks at him. They regard the tower which defies all Styrofoam odds. God watches.)*

The End

AYRAVANA FLIES OR A PRETTY DISH

by Sheila Callaghan

CHARACTERS

OLIVIA - 20s-30s, frizzy hair and bulgy eyes, a nervous sort
ELEPHANT - 30s-40s, crisp and well groomed, a bit delicate

SET

None.

ABOUT THE PRODUCTION

Originally produced by Sheila Callaghan & Christopher DeWan, for the Edge of the World Theater Festival, Nov. 8 - 18, 2001.

This play was performed during Vital Signs 10: New Works Festival at Vital Theatre Company, December 13 - 16, 2007 and was directed by David A. Miller. The cast included:

OLIVIA . . . . Lauren Walsh Singerman
ELEPHANT . . . . .Fletcher McTaggart

The 33rd Annual Samuel French Off Off Broadway Short Play Festival production of this play, directed by David A. Miller included the following people:

OLIVIA . . . . Lauren Walsh Singerman
ELEPHANT . . . . Rajiv Varma

ABOUT THE AUTHOR

Sheila's plays have been produced nationally and internationally (*Dead City, We Are Not These Hands* among others). Her play *Crawl, Fade To White* was produced by 13P in October 2008, and her play *That Pretty Pretty; or, The Rape Play* will be produced by Rattlestick in February 2009.

(**ELEPHANT** *and* **OLIVIA** *are standing in their own spaces.* **OLIVIA** *is wearing lipstick that is far too red.* **ELEPHANT** *is wearing a suit and tie. They both carry large suitcases.*)

OLIVIA. It was a pretty dish. A pretty pretty pretty pretty dish. Dish meaning meal of course. RECIPE. A pretty pretty recipe. Meant to be. Orchestrated as such. And EXOTIC. People like pretty and exotic things. Even if they are fleeting. If they fleet. ESPECIALLY if they fleet. And dishes of course fleet because one second they are sitting before you on a plate pretty as a petunia and in a blink they are muscled through your thorax and thrashed to oblivion by gastronomic juices.

ELEPHANT. I wasn't feeling very special at the time.

OLIVIA. Pretty dish with lots of colors. EXOTIC. Gloria darn it I have an idea and she looks at me like I've never had an idea in my life which isn't far from the truth for all she knows because original ideas don't come quickly in this little shoebox bistro with the dirt floor and net ceiling. I mean one can't possibly get a proper idea with all the airplanes roaring overhead. The noise, the outrageous obtrusive interminable NOISE of it! Every day, every hour…It would be different if we had a proper ceiling but we don't, all we have is a net, so we walk around in special shoes when it rains so we won't sink down into the mud…

ELEPHANT. I had a thunderous headache from the sound of airplanes overhead. It doesn't always bother me but for some reason that day I was excessively sensitive to my aural environment. I work at the airport, you see.

OLIVIA. Gloria darn it I have an idea and I skid over to her skid you see because it had been raining all morning and the floor was one big mud slick and Gloria looks at me with this FACE and I try to muster a twinkle in my eye to get her all anticipatory, build some tension you know, and then I say

ELEPHANT. Vegetable stew

OLIVIA. Vegetable stew

ELEPHANT. Vegetable stew

OLIVIA. Vegetable stew

ELEPHANT. Vegetable stew

OLIVIA. Vegetable stew

ELEPHANT. Vegetable stew

OLIVIA. Special of the day.

ELEPHANT. I wasn't feeling very special. My headache made me cross and mopey. So I decided to treat myself to lunch.

OLIVIA. Golden peppers I say. GOLDEN, I say, the valuable kind. And shiny, so shiny you can see the reflection of the crisscross patterns of the net ceiling on its skin. The sun had come out by then you see. But the floor was still muddy. Mud takes a while to dry. And big luscious tomatoes, I mean LUSCIOSO, the kind with the sweet pulpy tongues. Fat bawling onions with crispy skins. And fresh basil, stems and all. And something virile, like a zucchini, a big hard zucchini, so big and colossal it could choke an elephant.

(**OLIVIA** *and* **ELEPHANT** *glance ominously at each other.*)

ELEPHANT. I had never been to this bistro before. It was diminutive and ramshackle. The walls were cardboard. The floor was mud. My trouser cuffs were caked the moment I stepped in the door. And the ceiling was simply a stretched-out hairnet.

OLIVIA. Pretty dish, pretty pretty pretty dish. All the colors of fall. To remind people of the passing seasons, of their own mortality. Some universal pondering with their afternoon meal. Came to me in a flash, Gloria. Gloria? What do you think? Gloria smiles a full fleshy smile. The space between her eyebrows involuntarily twitches.

We trade eye twinkles…and then I really let her have it. CUMIN, I say. CUMIN? She asks, her entire face a question. Gloria, we've been Amerciana-Ordinaire for very very long time. Look around you. The couple in the corner snorting chicken soup through drinking straws…the businessman at the counter dripping candle wax onto his strip steak…the toad in the undershirt eating glass…they are desperate for a comestible adventure! All people really want in life is adventure. I say we give it to them.

Gloria is quiet for a moment. Then her bottom lip does a little quiver-dee-do, and she says OLIVIA which she never says because it's not my name, wait, sorry yes it is, OLIVIA, you are a genius.

ELEPHANT. I sat down by the window where the floor was most muddy from the morning showers and opened my menu. Then I went like this: eh, mm, na, woo, hun, ar. Because nothing really tickled my trunk.

OLIVIA. SO. Chop chop chop I go, dice dice dice chop, mix mix, taste, mix mix sprinkle sprinkle pour, mix mix taste, cook cook cook cook cook taste sprinkle cook cook cook cook taste scream swear, cook cook cook cook cook cook taste and smile. And I'm shuttled to another time and place, growing up as a little girl on the vegetable farm. No. Yes, the vegetable farm. In my Tom Sawyer overalls and my straw hat and my bare feet, skipping through the plantation and digging up vegetables from the warm soil, then skipping home with a full basket and cooking them all up in a big wicker pot, then adding special spices I'd ordered from my spice catalogue, exotic spices with names too long to pronounce, from countries too small to see, and I'd serve them warm in a loaf of bread with the heart torn out. Ooooooooh. Mmmmmmmm. La la la la la. People clamored at my kitchen window in frenzied hordes for a taste of my wildly original dishes. "Olivia is cooking in her wicker pot again, bring the tin foil and the toothpicks!" Tearing each other's hair, ripping their own shirts. For a TASTE, I tell you. And after one bite they'd drop to the dirt in a swoon. Because I made more than just dishes. I made VOODOO. Not the creepy kind with the mumbling and the eyes-rolled back and the rag doll stuck with pins. The good kind. I burned flavors into peoples mouth – memories. I could conjure music from the tip of the tongue to the uvula, each tiny increment of space resounding a different chord. It was clear I had a future as a Voodoo Priestess of Culinary Wizardry. But alas. I got thwarted somewhere between point A and point A. Until now.

ELEPHANT. Pardon me…

(OLIVIA *and* ELEPHANT *glance at each other.* OLIVIA *skids over to* ELEPHANT.)

She was a manic young lass. There was something spooked and gurgling about her. It was enchanting.

OLIVIA. I had never seen a pachyderm up close before. Not in a suit, at any rate. He had huge grey lashes and ancient pupils. His grey skin fell in thick folds above his collar. Was he a South African Bush elephant? A Malaysian Tree elephant? A Sri Lankan Marsh-hopper? Was he EXOTIC?

ELEPHANT. I'm a vegetarian.

OLIVIA. Where are you from?

ELEPHANT. I grew up in a small village in central India. But nowadays I consider myself more of a citizen of the world.

OLIVIA. Where do you work?

ELEPHANT. The airport.

(OLIVIA *gasps.*)

OLIVIA (*aside*) Exotic indeed! A true wayfarer!

ELEPHANT (*aside*) She was impressed, the saucy little beaver. My fat heart swelled. I asked her if she might tell me the special of the day.

OLIVIA. With pleasure.

ELEPHANT. The noise from the planes overhead was so

clamorous she had to lean in close to say it. Her hair smelled like pepper. Her breath was vague on my cheek. Her frizzy hairdo tickled my proboscis. She whispered...

OLIVIA. Vegetable stew

ELEPHANT. Vegetable stew

OLIVIA. Vegetable stew

ELEPHANT. Vegetable stew

OLIVIA. Vegetable stew

ELEPHANT. Vegetable stew

OLIVIA. With CUMIN.

(**ELEPHANT** *gasps.*)

ELEPHANT. A spice from home. It had been so long. Thoughts of the festival...the heat, the sitars, dust rising in clouds from my feet, jewels draped on dyed cloth hanging between my eyes, "Ayravana, Ayravana, Vahana of Indra, Vahana of Sakra..." They whispered their holy hymns into my ears....

OLIVIA (*to* **ELEPHANT**) I made it myself

ELEPHANT. "Ayravana...you've lost your wings...will you fly again...fly Ayravana..."

OLIVIA. It has shiny golden peppers and big luscious tomatoes...

ELEPHANT. I was transported...the dark men, their turbans wrapped tightly, their thick black beards pointing toward their hearts, the women in their kaleidoscoping saris and their jangling jewelry, all kneeling before me and singing the tale of my legacy:

(*singing*)

"Thousands of years ago, to the north of the Himalayas, a banyan tree of great height stood. One day, a flying elephant, while passing over the tree, swooped down and alighted upon one of its old branches to rest awhile. The old branch, unable to bear the massive weight of the elephant, at once crashed and fell. The hermit Dirghatapas had been seated beneath the tree engrossed in meditation and of course was unhappy to have been landed upon. He immediately cursed the elephant bird and deprived him of his wings, and so others of his kind. The elephant thus was forever earthbound."

OLIVIA. ...fat bawling onions and fresh basil....

ELEPHANT. This is the legend they sang as they placed the cool damp cloths to my temples and waved their colored plumes at my underside. And my answer to them? "Good people of India, fear not...I shall fly again."

But as I uttered this vow I knew it was a lie. Contrary to my robust appearance, I am timid beast. I resist adventure. I cringe at most derivations of titillation. I arrived in this country by sea, not by air, adding weeks to my journey to subvert the condition of airborne-osity. I work at the airport so I may be close to those who take flight, knowing all the while I have not the courage to join them.

OLIVIA. And a big hard zucchini.

ELEPHANT. And she. All tangles and tempestuousness. She'd not look upon me with such dewy eyes if she knew my true nature...I strained to disguise it. I ordered the special of the day with a hearty nod and a courageous roar. YES, YES, I BELIEVE I SHALL HAVE THE VEGETABLE STEW.

OLIVIA. Such force, such acumen, such conviction! I want to please this elephant like I had never wanted to please anyone before. I skid off to the kitchen and skid back with a plate of the prettiest meal this bistro had ever seen.

(OLIVIA *presents the dish to* ELEPHANT *with a fabulous flourish. She skids off and peers at him from around the corner as he inspects his food.*)

ELEPHANT. My, what a pretty dish.

(OLIVIA *squeals with joy.* ELEPHANT *snifs the food.*)

...home...

(ELEPHANT *begins to eat with gusto. All of a sudden*

he begins to gag. His gags become violent. He makes the universal symbol for choking.)

OLIVIA. He's choking!

ELEPHANT. Agggkkk

OLIVIA. What do I do?

ELEPHANT. I saw a life flash before me. But it wasn't mine. It was the life of Ayravana, the elephant bird, flying from adventure to adventure, his thin wide ears ruddering the winds, over desert over forest over sea, racing beside the great metal flying machines, the brave and true Ayravana whose only sin was being too heavy, and I vowed to myself if I ever breathed another breath I would be that Aravana. I would swallow my terror and take to the sky. I would keep my promise to India. And I would learn to chew my food better.

(ELEPHANT continues to choke.)

OLIVIA. Gloria isn't around…the lunch crowd is gone…I don't know the Heimlick maneuver…His skin is turning white. His trunk is curling. He's at the mercy of an instrument of death fashioned by my own hand! My own pretty dish turned weapon of destruction. It shall not be!

I rush over to him having no clue what to do once I get there, and in my haste my feet lose their friction and I skid across the bistro through the mud slick, trip over a table leg and land head first into the belly of the elephant.

(She does so. A large green vegetable flies from ELE-PHANT's mouth. He gasps for air. OLIVIA retrieves the vegetable from the floor. It is an enormous zucchini. OLIVIA and ELEPHANT gaze at each other.)

ELEPHANT. My life

OLIVIA. My future

ELEPHANT. My past

OLIVIA. My love

ELEPHANT. A flight

OLIVIA. Exotic

ELEPHANT. A flight

OLIVIA. Exotic

ELEPHANT. A flight

OLIVIA. Exotic

ELEPHANT. An exotic flight.

(They touch hands.)

I made a phone call later that hour. Used all my free miles, the perks of being an airport employee, and booked a passage to anywhere. Leaving tomorrow in the A.M. Two tickets.

(ELEPHANT and OLIVIA look lovingly at each other.)

OLIVIA. I say goodbye to Gloria. I pack. Some clothes, an empty spice rack, and my spice-collecting tool kit. I clear my head and cleanse my palate. I buy a journal to keep a record off all the flavors that await my mouth. I ready my spirit for adventure.

(They take hold of their suitcases.)

ELEPHANT. I dream that night of a blue sky embrace, of most mist on my eyelids, of soft Indian chants growing distant as the air lifts me weightless on its clean breath.

OLIVIA. I dream that night of the prettiest dish ever, filled with colors that have no names, spices that have no country, seeping flavors that continue to anoint the tongue long after the food has been swallowed…I dream of lying face-up on a long slice of roasted eggplant in a large tomato-based broth, my head buzzing with all things flavorful…I dream into the future of my culinary story, of forging past zucchinis and peppers and onions and squash, of charging bravely into the underexplored territory of meats…the flesh of strange fowl and beast, of snake and eagle and donkey and sparrow, my mission to unveil all the palatary delights of otherwise untasted tertiary and/or air-based creatures…

(She glances hungrily at **ELEPHANT**, *devising elephant recipes in her mind.* **ELEPHANT** *glances shyly back, mistaking her hunger for lust.)*

OLIVIA. *(cont.)* Or, perhaps, a rare combination of both.

(A plane roars loudly overhead, so loudly it is almost deafening, and for a long time. **OLIVIA** *and* **ELEPHANT** *grit their teeth and hold their heads as it passes. It passes. They smile. Hold hands. Lights slowly fade.)*

The End

THE THREAD MEN

by Thomas C. Dunn

CHARACTERS

JOHN COLLINS - a psychiatrist, late 40s to 50s
ADDELIN LEWIS - late 20s to 30s

SET

An elevator.

TIME

The present.

ABOUT THE PRODUCTION

The 33rd Annual Samuel French Off Off Broadway Short Play Festival production of this play included the following people:

ADDELIN LEWIS . . . . Victor Verhaeghe
JOHN COLLINS . . . . Larry Block

Director: Richard Masur
Producer: Mark Borkowski
Production Company: Dream Theater (Artistic Director, Andrea Leigh)

The cast of the original workshop performance, directed by Thomas C. Dunn, included:

ADDELIN LEWIS . . . . Kenny Johnson
JOHN COLLINS . . . . Hugh Holub

ABOUT THE AUTHOR

Thomas C. Dunn's plays have been shown from New York to Los Angeles. In 2005, Dunn co-founded the film production company, Dream7 Entertainment, under which he co-wrote and directed *The Perfect Witness*, starring Wes Bentley. It was released by First Look Studios in February 2008. His next film, a thriller, is set to shoot in Spring of 2009.

(The elevator doors open and **JOHN** *enters.* **ADDELIN** *is already inside. The doors close and the elevator begins its descent. Suddenly, the lights darken, there is a loud rubbing noise and the elevator jars to a stop.* **JOHN** *reaches out and presses the lobby button.)*

ADDELIN. I already hit the lobby button.

JOHN. I can see that. But the elevator stopped.

ADDELIN. It's just that end of the day elevator ride. You know, when you want to get home, the ride seems so long you feel like you're dropping to the center of the earth.

JOHN. Well that's a plausible explanation also, but I think we've definitely stopped.

*(***ADDELIN*** *nods.* **JOHN** *continues hitting the lobby button. Nothing happens.)*

ADDELIN. Seems the lobby's not an option anymore.

JOHN. I'll just hit a different floor. When it opens we can take the stairs the rest of the way.

*(***JOHN*** *presses the other buttons.)*

ADDELIN. Why aren't the other buttons lighting up now?

JOHN. Maybe there's a power shortage. No, we still have lights.

ADDELIN. Well! My name is Addelin.

*(***ADDELIN*** *holds out his hand.* **JOHN** *doesn't see it.)*

My hand.

JOHN. *(distracted)* What?

*(***JOHN*** *notices his hand and they shake.)*

John. John Collins.

(beat)

Listen. Maybe we should sound the alarm, huh?

ADDELIN. Definitely. Sound the alarm.

JOHN. But I don't know…what happens…I mean what happens…when you do that?

ADDELIN. Well, I'd imagine that little button marked alarm would be depressed momentarily, then a bunch of bells ring and people coming racing to free you…like rats to a piece of cheese.

JOHN. Well, we'll press it. I mean…we're obviously stuck. So we'll just –

ADDELIN. Press…the…button.

(JOHN *presses the button. Nothing happens.*)

You see? It doesn't even work.

(JOHN *pulls out his cell phone.*)

JOHN. There's no…You getting a signal on your cell phone?

ADDELIN. What cell phone?

(beat)

Well take a seat, John. You're not claustrophobic, are you? Not afraid of being locked up…in a small place?

JOHN. No, I'm…actually a psychiatrist.

ADDELIN. A psychiatrist? Wow. You must be a pretty smart guy then, huh? That's good. I mean if I have to be closed up in a little cage with someone, it might as well be someone I can hold a decent conversation with, right, John?

(laughs hysterically)

So in your, uh, your profession, you would probably help people with, you know, problems like this.

JOHN. Being stuck in an elevator? You know, oddly enough, I don't get that problem too much.

ADDELIN. *(not amused)* That's funny, John. But what I meant is that you, as a psychiatrist, probably help people deal with life or death situations like this.

JOHN. Life or death? Listen, shouldn't we do something else? Try…

ADDELIN. What do you have in mind, John?

JOHN. We could yell.

ADDELIN. Yell? Go ahead, scream your head off.

JOHN. *(a soft yell)* Help. Help. Hellooooo. Help.

ADDELIN. I'm going to teach you how to scream, John. The trick is, if you're going to do it, give it a little…

(screams at the top of his lungs)

…LIFE! I was wondering if there'd be an echo…

JOHN. Perhaps the alarm is silent…

ADDELIN. Yeah, well, perhaps.

(Beat. JOHN continues looking about the elevator.)

Look, either the night custodians will come by later or when this place is flooded with people early tomorrow morning, they'll find us.

JOHN. *(to himself)* Looking like a couple of fools. Was there an 'out of order' sign on this elevator?

ADDELIN. John, if I had seen one, would I be in the elevator?

JOHN. I'm going to try to pry these doors open.

(JOHN moves toward the doors, then turns sharply on ADDELIN.)

Some people view being stuck in an elevator as very serious and have more important things to do then wait around for cleaning people and make jokes.

ADDELIN. You haven't made any jokes, John. Ohhhhh. You would be included in that 'some people' category. I'm sorry. I didn't even catch that. John, I'm just trying to bring a little lightness to a tense situation.

JOHN. What you are bringing is aggravation to an aggravating situation.

ADDELIN. Elevators like these have safety devices. They won't open between floors. We're just going to have to wait, John. Wait waitwaitwaitwaitwaitwait…

(ADDELIN continues to say "wait." JOHN massages his eyes and then suddenly glares at ADDELIN who notices the look and stops repeating. Beat.)

So! Tell me about yourself. Are you a family man John?

JOHN. Humh? Oh, uh yeah.

ADDELIN. Kids?

JOHN. No. Well I…No.

ADDELIN. 'Kids?' 'No. Well I…No.' That's an interesting answer John. So you never had kids?

JOHN. No.

ADDELIN. If you ever had a kid, what would you name it?

JOHN. What kind of question…? Michael.

ADDELIN. Michael. No middle name?

JOHN. *(shrugging)* Steven.

ADDELIN. Michael Steven…Collins. That's a nice name. That's the name of a kid who would be successful, you know, do his father proud. Probably be a psychologist like you.

JOHN. Psychiatrist.

ADDELIN. Well, psychiatrist then. Point is that's the name of a winner. Michael Steven Collins. I mean, you wouldn't find a kid with a name like that hanging out in some back alley or –

JOHN. I'd really rather not dwell on the subject of imaginary children.

ADDELIN. How about make-believe pets then?

(growls and barks at **JOHN***)*

I'm just kidding, John. Don't be so somber. It's a joke.

JOHN. I think perhaps –

ADDELIN. What?!

JOHN. – it would be better if we didn't talk.

ADDELIN. *(grabbing his chest as if wounded)* The silent treatment, huh? Ah, an old psychiatric stand-by. Not a very mature approach though.

JOHN. I am not giving you the silent treatment. I just think perhaps it would be better, if we cannot carry on an interesting conversation, to just keep quiet.

ADDELIN. *(overlapping)* I thought the conversation was interesting!

*(***JOHN*** glares at him.)*

At least mildly amusing if not full on interesting.

(JOHN *glares harder.*)

I'm sorry, John. Maybe you're right.

(beat)

Do you mind if I play some music?

(JOHN *looks at* ADDELIN *and around the elevator. There is obviously nothing that could possibly make music.*)

JOHN. No. Go right ahead.

ADDELIN. Jazz or Rock N' Roll?

JOHN. How are you going to play any…? Never mind. Never mind. Jazz is great.

ADDELIN. Jazz it is. Good selection.

(ADDELIN *begins playing drums, bass, trumpet, etc. with only his mouth*)

You know that one, John.

(continues music)

If you've got a particular favorite you'd like to hear just let me know. I can play anything.

(continues music)

I know "Blue Moon" like the back of my hand.

(ADDELIN*'s music becomes louder, more obnoxious.*)

JOHN. *(exploding)* Can you please stop playing…mouthing…can you stop making noise?!

ADDELIN. Oh. Oh. You're a Rock n' Roll man. You know I thought I had you pegged for a Rocker. Just wanted to seem sophisticated but deep down, Zeppelin, maybe even a little Sex Pistols. Okay, here we go.

(Mouths a heavy drum beat and electric guitar, holding an ear-piercing note.)

JOHN. PLEASE! STOP!

(ADDELIN *abruptly stops, pulls out a pack of cigarettes. He taps a cigarette's filter on the pack.* JOHN *turns and stares in disbelief.*)

ADDELIN. Mind if I smoke?

JOHN. In an elevator?

ADDELIN. As long as you don't mind.

(*puts the cigarette in his mouth*)

JOHN. I do mind! Maybe you should start coming to see me once a week. Or twice a week. Or better yet, I know an excellent psychiatrist way across town I can set you up with.

ADDELIN. I've already seen you, John.

(*There is a dead silence. The unlit cigarette hangs from* **ADDELIN**'s *lips.*)

I mean in the newspaper or something. You look very familiar. You even kind of look like some guy I used to know.

JOHN. Really? Who?

ADDELIN. Just some guy. He didn't know me real well. Could see me in the street, he'd walk right past me. Don't you think that's strange, John? The way people don't really notice each other. The way everyone's just shadows in a dim world. And no one really tries to shed light on these shadows, try to see them for what they are, understand them.

(**ADDELIN** *flicks at his lighter, trying to get the cigarette lit.*)

JOHN. The cigarette.

ADDELIN. You want one?

JOHN. Please don't light it.

ADDELIN. Oh right. Sorry.

(**ADDELIN** *pockets the lighter, slides the unlit cigarette back into the pack.*)

It's fucking strange, John. It's fucking strange. I mean people's lives are so connected and yet they go through their lives like they're…falling down an elevator shaft and they only have time to fall from top to bottom with no time to grab hold and stop. But maybe, if they're lucky, right before they fall, they notice the person they're in the elevator with. Really...see who it is, you know? Then there might be a little bit of hope, a little bit. Then we're not just falling through life, we're living it.

(JOHN *focuses intently on* ADDELIN, *the coincidence of the analogy not lost on him.*)

JOHN. I don't think I caught your name.

ADDELIN. I told you.

JOHN. *(nervous laughter)* I was so caught up in the elevator being stuck and all, it's slipped away. Your name?

ADDELIN. Addelin.

JOHN. Addelin. Addelin. Last name?

ADDELIN. Lewis. Addelin Lewis.

(JOHN *steps forward, his arms crossed, thinking.*)

JOHN. *(trying to remember)* Addelin Lewis. Addelin Lewis.

(ADDELIN *steps forward, his arms crossed, mirroring* JOHN.)

ADDELIN. Mean anything to you?

JOHN. I don't know. Should it?

(JOHN *searches* ADDELIN'*s face for an answer.* ADDELIN *stares back; their eyes lock. They are both completely still.*)

Sounds like I've heard it before.

ADDELIN. Well this gets back to what I was saying. We've probably met somewhere and never noticed each other. I thought you were in the paper. You weren't in the paper, a few months back?

JOHN. No. I wasn't in the paper.

ADDELIN. Well who knows then, right? We probably have donuts at the same donut shop.

(They both lower their eyes. Some light laughter.)

JOHN. Yes. What do you do for a living, Mr. uh, Lewis?

ADDELIN. I'm an elevator repairman.

JOHN. What?

ADDELIN. I'm an elevator repairman.

JOHN. What are you kidding?

ADDELIN. Nope.

JOHN. I'm stuck in an elevator with an elevator repairman?

ADDELIN. Boy, that is ironic, huh?

JOHN. I don't believe this. You're an elevator repairman. It's like your car breaks down in the desert and after an hour, the hitchhiker you picked up tells you he's a fucking mechanic... and he's never even opened the hood of the car to see what's wrong.

(ADDELIN bursts into laughter.)

Or...or you're starving in Siberia somewhere and after eight days your friend turns to you and says...and says...we could always eat these sandwiches in my bag.

ADDELIN. Sandwiches in the bag...

(ADDELIN's laughter has a contagious effect on JOHN who reluctantly begins chuckling too. Soon, both are in hysterics.)

JOHN. Oh God. Oh. OH. So! If you're an elevator repairman, why, pray tell, did you not fix the goddamn elevator?

ADDELIN. *(barely able to contain himself long enough to speak)* Because...I'm the one who rigged the elevator...so we would get stuck here in the first place!

(ADDELIN continues laughing. JOHN laughs for a split second and then is suddenly dead serious. ADDELIN looks straight-faced at JOHN.)

I'm just kidding!

(ADDELIN bursts into new peals of laughter. The thrill of the moment is obviously gone for JOHN.)

JOHN. But you are an elevator technician of some sort. Yes?

ADDELIN. Yes.

JOHN. Then why don't you figure out how to get us out of here?

ADDELIN. Look at the sign. Should the elevator doors fail to open, do not become alarmed.

(overlapping)

Remain in elevator until assistance arrives. DO NOT attempt to force the doors or emergency escape hatch open.

JOHN. *(overlapping)* Yes. But that's talking about the average person. That doesn't refer to someone who's job it is to fix these things.

ADDELIN. Please use button marked 'Alarm' to summon aid.

JOHN. We tried that.

ADDELIN. Elevator companies are on call twenty-four hours a day.

JOHN. What good is that if they don't know we're in here?

ADDELIN. They will know, John. They will know. Wait until the cleaning crew gets to the nineteenth floor.

JOHN. Why should we wait if...the...what?

ADDELIN. Wait until –

JOHN. The nineteenth floor? That's the floor I got in on.

ADDELIN. Yeah? So?

JOHN. The elevator moved when I first got on. I mean...we moved! I thought it was almost at the lobby.

ADDELIN. John. John. John. When an elevator's cable gets too old or for one reason or another, some of the cable snaps, the elevator still tries to run along the cables...

(mouths 'rusty cable' noises)

...thereby giving the illusion that the elevator is going down. This elevator actually only moved a few feet.

JOHN. So you're telling me we're suspended nineteen floors up in an elevator with old, broken cables?

(JOHN paces. ADDELIN jumps up and down as if testing the stability of the elevator.)

ADDELIN. Eighteenth or nineteenth I would say. Look, I'd try to fix it but even if I did get to the cable, I don't have the tools to do anything about it. We just have to wait and try to relax.

JOHN. Relax? I just found out my life is in jeopardy.

ADDELIN. Your life is always in jeopardy, John. Sometimes you're just more aware of it.

JOHN. Well that's very helpful, thanks for that!

ADDELIN. Seriously, you look tense as all hell. You're pacing back and forth like...an expectant father. Boy, that must be an experience, huh? Waiting for your kid to be born. I can't imagine anything as nerve-wracking. No. Well, maybe two things. Your wedding day, right? And if you knew that your life was at the mercy of some-one else and there was nothing you could do about it. That's nerve wracking. Were you...uh...tense...when your kid was being born, John?

JOHN. Excuse me?

ADDELIN. When your boy was born, were you tense? I mean everyone's tense but...tell me what it felt like, hanging out in the waiting room.

(JOHN stares at ADDELIN for a moment, trying to focus his thoughts.)

JOHN. It wasn't too bad. You just try to stay calm the best you can.

ADDELIN. Yeah?

JOHN. You get some coffee, thumb through magazines, try to think about...what you can do, in the future, to make your kid live a good, productive life. How you're going to mold him...

ADDELIN. I'd imagine you'd be thinking about whether the baby will be healthy or not.

JOHN. Well yes Addeline, of course –

ADDELIN. Addelin.

JOHN. What?

ADDELIN. Addelin.

JOHN. That's what I sa –

ADDELIN. No. You said Addeline. My name is Addelin.

JOHN. Addelin!

ADDELIN. Right! But you know John, how are you supposed to know if you're going to raise your kid right?
I mean, you could do everything a father possibly can
and what's to say the kid's not going to grow up to be
some…I don't know…some…I'm pulling this out of
a hat…drug addict, or something? Am I right, John?
What's your kid do again? He's probably, what, still in
college?

JOHN. He's in college.

ADDELIN. I figured. What college is that, John?

JOHN. Look. I'm kind of tired. I don't want to…do these…
things…

ADDELIN. 'These…things'…What college? John, are you
okay?

JOHN. *(exploding)* Yes! Leave me alone, all right? Can I just
stand here for two fucking minutes without having your
questions pounding into my head? I'm trapped in an
elevator with a fucking elevator technician who won't
try to fix it because the sign says not to, so instead, he
tries his hand at amateur talk show host.

*(During JOHN's tirade ADDELIN reaches into his coat
pocket, removes a water and drinks.)*

ADDELIN. I'm no psychologist –

JOHN. Psychiatrist!

ADDELIN. – but that display doesn't seem like very normal
behavior to me, John.

JOHN. *(yelling)* Can we have just a few minutes without
talking?!

ADDELIN. SURE!

*(There is complete silence for about twenty seconds.
ADDELIN begins to play "Blue Moon" by making trumpet sounds with his mouth.)*

I told you I could play it.

(*continues music*)

I was just getting to know you, John. I think it's important to know a person before you pass judgment on them.

JOHN. Before you what?

ADDELIN. Do you have the time?

JOHN. Twenty to midnight.

(**ADDELIN** *checks his own watch.*)

ADDELIN. Good. Good.

JOHN. You have a watch.

ADDELIN. I never said I didn't.

JOHN. You strike me as a very dark person.

ADDELIN. (*laughing*) Is that a professional opinion? You want to know dark, John? Let me explain it to you. As a little kid I grew up with my grandparents and around five, six years old, my grandfather got sick. The doctor said bronchitis. My grandmother gave him some medicine but he still had this...hacking cough. That's not even it. This cough was like...the scraping of your insides. My grandfather would just lay in bed screaming between coughs that there was some goddamn hair spray in his throat. He was convinced that someone in the house was filling his room with hair spray every time he fell asleep. Well, for the first week, you know, my grandmother, my two aunts who lived with us, they wouldn't go near hair spray or any kind of spray, out of concern. But two weeks later my grandfather's still coughing and coughing and telling them he can't even breathe. But what are they going to do, right? Not use spray bottles to clean the house? Let their hair go to shit? So a little spray here and there. Within two weeks, they're spraying it on thick, telling him to shut up, that it's all in his mind. So that's it. All that pain is in his mind. His whole lower face is covered with phlegm and drool because he's tired of wiping it off. His body's slick with sweat and his stomach is distorted. You know the muscles, from contracting and contracting, night and day…they're just bulging out of this emaciated body. And he's screaming fucking bloody murder, 'the hair spray, the hair spray.' But the pain's in his mind, so they just ignore him. When I found him the doctor said he'd been dead for two days, suffocated on some combination of phlegm and vomit. It was probably the paint on the walls or…they denied him his suffering and dignity in death because they couldn't understand the pain. They couldn't see it, they couldn't feel it, so they just convinced themselves it shouldn't be there at all.

(The next line should not be delivered callously. **JOHN** *is affected emotionally. Oftentimes, our truer expressions of sympathy are reduced to such generic expressions.)*

JOHN. People can't always be perfect. They –

ADDELIN. People-can't-always-be-perfect. Well thank you, that sheds a whole new light on that little family tragedy –

JOHN. I just mean that people are sometimes going to do terrible things but you have to judge them on their potential to change, their interest in bettering themselves –

ADDELIN. Sonuvabitch.

JOHN. What?

ADDELIN. Did you just say 'by their interest in bettering themselves?'

JOHN. Yes. I think that's very important.

ADDELIN. You think that's important? Your thought, then, would be a professional opinion…since you are…a psychiatrist, right? You're able to judge how to live life and how not to live it…you set the moral guidelines of human beings, don't you?

JOHN. I think that's an inflated definition of what we actually do –

ADDELIN. I think you believe in that inflated definition –

JOHN. And I don't think you know me well enough to say what my beliefs are –

ADDELIN. But you know me well enough to say what mine are. I know you a lot better than you think, John. It's unbelievable that you don't know me.

JOHN. Why would I know you, Addeline?

ADDELIN. John, my name is Addelin, okay? Just, you know, try to pronounce it right.

JOHN. I'm sick of waiting in this fucking elevator.

(He checks his cell phone for a signal again. Nothing.)

I'm going to find out who's responsible for it breaking down and sue his ass, for what I would charge, by the hour, for a patient. This is really outrageous.

ADDELIN. It's unjust.

JOHN. Damn right it's unjust. We've been suspended on some broken cables who knows how high up –

ADDELIN. The eighteenth or nineteenth floor –

JOHN. – with our lives in danger. And now I'm sweating.

ADDELIN. They turn off the air conditioning at night –

JOHN. This damn thing is so hot!

ADDELIN. You're married, right?

JOHN. You know, you have this incredible knack for asking ridiculous questions at completely inappropriate times.

ADDELIN. I didn't know there were appropriate times for ridiculous questions. And I didn't know 'are you married' was a ridiculous question –

JOHN. It is when you're suspended twenty floors up in a broken elevator.

ADDELIN. Well could you give me some sort of guideline for the right questions to ask in this situation?

JOHN. I'M DIVORCED!

ADDELIN. *(laughs slowly at first, then hilariously)* Divorced? That's even better. You're a divorced psychiatrist.

JOHN. There's something wrong with you.

ADDELIN. Don't fucking tell me there's something wrong with me you self-righteous sonuvabitch. Who gave you the power to judge someone's sanity?

JOHN. I do know you, don't I?

ADDELIN. No. You don't know me at all. But you met me.

JOHN. When? Where do I know you from? Were you a patient?

ADDELIN. You're mighty concerned now, John, aren't you? You're mighty concerned now.

JOHN. *(overlapping; yelling)* Where do I know you from?

ADDELIN. Well, we have to drag up some memories, John. Do you, by any chance, remember…the name Gabriella Lewis?

JOHN. No. I don't remember the name –

ADDELIN. You didn't even try.

JOHN. I don't remember. Was she your wife?

ADDELIN. *(with an imaginary microphone)* Excellent guess. Give the man a prize. What do we have for John today…

    (indicating **JOHN***)*

…Dick? Well, Addeline, John's got a night's vacation in a five star elevator in a plush downtown skyscraper. Well aren't you the lucky fucking man? Yeah. She was. But she's not anybody now.

JOHN. Did she die?

ADDELIN. You don't know?

JOHN. Why do you keep talking to me like I'm involved in your life?

ADDELIN. Oh, that's right. You wouldn't know if she's dead because you've been mixing up the living with the dead all night long.

JOHN. What are you talking about? Tell me what the fuck is going on here or, so help me, I'll…I'll…

ADDELIN. Apart from that being very unconvincing, John, it's also not a very professional attitude.

JOHN. *(overlapping)* Tell me right now who you are and what you're talking about!

ADDELIN. *(overlapping)* John, this conversation's getting tense. Maybe…we should listen to a little elevator music. All we need is my mouth.

(mouths a few notes…)

JOHN. I'm warning you!

ADDELIN. You're warning me? I'm being threatened? But at the same time I've got another burning question in my mind that I've just got to ask. What kind of man thinks he can unravel the human mind and solve it like a jigsaw puzzle when he can't even keep his own marriage together? The divorced psychiatrist. Boy, that's ironic –

*(**JOHN** finally has been put over the edge between the endless questions and mystery, his containment, and the intense heat of the elevator. He punches **ADDELIN** hard in the stomach and **ADDELIN** drops to his knees.)*

(trying hard to recover his wind; suddenly beginning to laugh) I've got another question John. What…psychiatrist lets…lets his own son overdose on drugs. That's right, John. I know all about it. Your life! I read the story in the newspaper. The one you weren't even in.

JOHN. I told you –

ADDELIN. You told me you didn't have a kid, then you have a kid and he's in college, but he's dead! Obsolete, gone, skull and bones in the dirt dead! It's in the newspaper how he died. He fucking heroin overdosed in the back of an alley –

JOHN. Shut the fuck up, you sadistic bastard! How did I ever get stuck here with…you set this up. An elevator technician, you set this up. You sick bastard. Who are you?!

*(**JOHN** pounds **ADDELIN** on the back with his fists, screaming 'who are you?' Finally exhausted, **JOHN** backs off, wiping the sweat from his brow, while **ADDELIN** slowly gains his composure and raises himself to his feet. **ADDELIN** begins to mouth Rossini's "Barber Of Seville.")*

ADDELIN. I'll tell you where you were, John, when your kid, Michael Steven Collins, was dying. You were talking about competence and ink blots and...bullshit...You were out evaluating me and saying, and I quote...here, I wrote it down.

(**ADDELIN** *pulls an old piece of paper from his pocket, unfolds it and reads. Halfway through, he stops looking at the paper. It is obviously well memorized.*)

"I feel that at this time Addeline Lewis should be kept here for further evaluation. His past record indicates that he uses violence as a means of rectifying what he considers 'injustice.' I see no interest in the patient in bettering himself in the various programs open to him, and most important, no acknowledgment of what he did as wrong. I must conclude, therefore, that without this basic understanding, he is unable to peacefully coexist in society..."

(**ADDELIN** *places the paper in* **JOHN**'s *shirt pocket.*)

Let me take this golden opportunity to explain something to you, John. When a man rapes your wife, that's injustice. Justice is that man's death and it is not wrong to put a knife through that man's chest. I tried twice to kill the man who raped my wife...who took her life... and it was taking her life, John. Rape took her life and left the shell.

JOHN. What do you want me to do about that now?

ADDELIN. Don't say a fucking word! How's that? After the rape...the person, the magic, that was my wife was gone. She kept picturing him around her, thinking about her...he lived in the same building, John. I'd see him checking his mail. Bill. Bill. Bill. The police, the courts, were dragging it out and I couldn't stand seeing her suffer because that bastard had wanted a few minutes of pleasure...pleasure, is that what it is? I spent three years undergoing psychiatric evaluation, on your recommendation, for trying to kill him. He ended up going to jail for two years, John. Out on parole and he raped again...probably a few more times they don't even know about. And you know why?

Because you thought at the time when he came around for parole that, let me guess, he was showing, "great interest in the various programs open to him." He did the same thing again, John, raped another woman… and while I'm reading about it in the papers, sitting in a room the size of this elevator, I just kept thinking how strange it was that you evaluated us both. You… who can't stop your own life from crumbling –

JOHN. Shut up! Shut up!

ADDELIN. You, who even on seeing me, can't remember me. Locked in an elevator with the man you declared three years ago was insane! And you don't even know me! You still pronounce my name wrong. You don't even know my name.

JOHN. I remember you now. You've had your say.

(JOHN *slowly composes himself and puts on his overcoat as if preparing to leave. He stands directly in front of the doors, waiting.* ADDELIN *simply stares.*)

Now open these doors.

(ADDELIN *observes him for a few moments.*)

ADDELIN. That's it? You don't even ask me why I did this? Let me guess, because in that great mind of yours, you've already got it figured out. Well if this conclusion is anything like your others, you're way off the mark. So let me just spell it out for you, John. I brought you here…on the nineteenth floor…so I could show you something about the soul of a person, John. Not the mind. The soul. I don't think you're getting this, John. You're showing no interest in bettering yourself. I must conclude therefore, that without this basic understanding –

JOHN. Open these damn doors now!

ADDELIN. – you are unable to peacefully coexist with society!

JOHN. I swear to God, if you don't open these damn doors –

ADDELIN. What God do you have to swear to? There's only one way out for you, John, and that's down, free-falling straight down through the fucking lobby.

JOHN. What are you saying?

ADDELIN. Oh John. Do you have the time?

JOHN. What are you saying?

ADDELIN. What time is it?

JOHN. Tell me what the fuck –

ADDELIN. The time John!

JOHN. 11:55, you sonuvabitch!

ADDELIN. *(checking his own watch)* You sonuvabitch! 11:56. John, come midnight the cables suspending this elevator will no longer be in operation. I've made the arrangements for them to release in four minutes –

JOHN. You're full of shit. You're bluffing.

ADDELIN. Am I? I read the article on your son, got confidential copies of your psychiatric recommendations for both myself and the rapist of my wife...and I studied your daily schedule inside and out. I rewired this elevator and disabled the safety mechanisms so I could catch you like a rat in a trap. So don't fool yourself for one second into thinking I'm bluffing. I've worked too hard to see your face contort as it falls and when this elevator floor comes crashing up through your skull when we hit the lobby.

JOHN. You're a madman. You're –

ADDELIN. Just like I was when you first evaluated me, John, insane to the point of violence when seeking justice. You shouldn't have passed my case along, John. Maybe you could've helped me.

JOHN. Let me out right now or I am warning you –

ADDELIN. Do you understand? Boom! In three minutes, we both die. If you want to beat me some more for the last three minutes of your life, then do it but I would think you'd have other priorities.

(turning away from **JOHN** *and quietly praying)*

Hail Mary, full of grace,

The Lord is with Thee

Blessed art thou among women

And blessed is the fruit of thy womb Jesus

(overlapping)

Holy Mary, Mother of God, pray for us sinners…

JOHN. *(overlapping)* If this elevator drops, you're going to die too.

ADDELIN. *(cont.)* Now and at the hour of our death.

(**ADDELIN** *spreads his arms like Jesus on the cross.*)

I'm resigned to my fate though.

JOHN. Are you? Is your need for vengeance so strong that you would sacrifice your own life to take mine? Don't you think your life is worth more than that? Don't you think…Gabriella…deserves, needs you more now?

ADDELIN. Don't talk about her –

JOHN. Gabriella.

ADDELIN. Don't –

JOHN. Gabriella!

ADDELIN. Shut up! You don't know a thing about her. And as for my life, John, well you ended that a long time ago. Three years in a mental institution. That's longer than I was married at the time. And I had to leave my beautiful wife to struggle through the abyss alone… I've got no life worth keeping.

JOHN. Give yourself a second chance. Give me a second chance…We're both capable of change.

ADDELIN. Do you think so?

JOHN. I do. I really do. The only thing in our way is these doors. So if you can open them, then open them. I won't press charges. Not with all…all that I've done to you in the past. You've had enough suffering. Let's put all that suffering behind us.

ADDELIN. Then what do we do after we finally accept all the suffering?

JOHN. We move on. We move on. But first the doors. Open the doors.

ADDELIN. Do you really feel like you've understood...something here, John?

JOHN. *(overlapping)* I've learned a lot. I was wrong, Addeline. I was...out of line...Addelin. I was completely wrong. I see it now. The injustice of it all...how cruel it must have been for you...but right now we need to open these doors.

ADDELIN. I'm thinking about what you're saying, John, and I'm just having a little trouble...believing your psychiatric crisis situation bullshit so just spare me your insincerity. I told you I'm teaching you a lesson about the soul, you dense prick. Don't talk to me about understanding. You had your chance for that.

(The elevator jolts.)

That's it, John. That's the sign. One more minute.

*(**ADDELIN** keeps repeating 'tic' over **JOHN**'s next lines)*

JOHN. All I did was...making a decision that I thought would be best, your best interest...it seemed...cases often...with so many other things to consider...

ADDELIN. John, you're faltering. You're babbling. This isn't any way for God to be acting –

JOHN. I'm not God!

ADDELIN. Well you're going to have to be right now.

JOHN. Please...don't let this happen.

*(**JOHN** keeps repeating the word "please")*

ADDELIN. John, you'd kill me right now if it would do you any good, wouldn't you? You'd kill the man who is causing what you consider a terrible injustice. Wouldn't you, John? Come on, John. We drop like a falling star in...forty-two seconds. Would you kill me? You can say it. Come on, John! Would you kill me?! COME ON, JOHN!

JOHN. *(completely losing it)* GOD...YES! I'D KILL YOU! I'D KILL YOU...Just don't let this happen!

ADDELIN. How can you judge me? How can you judge anyone? Look at what you are…

(**JOHN** *collapses in the corner, clutching his legs to his chest, sobbing.*)

What are your last words, John? What's the last thing you ever want to say on this earth?

JOHN. Mercy…stop it from happening…under…under…stand…

ADDELIN. I understand it all, John. Those are your last words? A pleading for your life? What about some sort of remorse… repentance…John, your body is going to drop but maybe your soul…can rise.

(**JOHN** *is too hysterical to talk.* **ADDELIN** *checks his watch.*) Four…three…two…one…

(**JOHN** *screams out desperately.*)

…zero.

(*During* **JOHN**'s *scream, the elevator darkens and moves downwards one foot. It was always a foot above the lobby. The doors open.* **ADDELIN** *steps out.*)

I want you to remember, John. I don't want you to ever forget this suffering, how you just screamed…that was the scream of the son you never heard…and my wife who you never saw, never felt for…that scream, John… is the piercing of your soul.

(*There is just the sound of* **JOHN**'s *staggered breathing, light whimpering.* **ADDELIN** *moves offstage. The elevator doors close as the lights fade to black.*)

The End

THE DYING BREED

by Thomas Higgins

CHARACTERS

MARK

PAULA

ABOUT THE PRODUCTION

The 33rd Annual Samuel French Off Off Broadway Short Play Festival production of this play included the following people:

MARK (first performance) . . . . Norbert Leo Butz

MARK (second performance) . . . . Neal Huff

PAULA . . . . Michelle Federer

Director: Laura Savia

ABOUT THE AUTHOR

Thomas Higgins is the author of *The Blasphemy Tree* (Naked Angels Lab), *The Family Dungeon* (Columbia Arts Initiative), *The Home Front* (Columbia University Arts Initiative), and *The Wild Life* (Source Theatre in DC). His play, *This Modern House*, was nominated for the 2007 Cherry Lane Mentor Project and the 2007 L. Arnold Weissberger Award at Williamstown. *The Elephant Party* was nominated for the 2008 Cherry Lane Mentor Project and *The Home Maker* was just read at The Atlantic Theatre Company as part of the NUEA NU Works Reading Series. He graduated from Northwestern University, where he was named a Walton Theatre Scholar and received the T. Stephen May Scriptwriting Award. He recently received his MFA in Playwriting at Columbia University on the Dean's Fellowship.

(**MARK** *and* **PAULA**, *on a bench in a dog park.*)

(**PAULA** *wears a macabre expression;* **MARK**, *a slightly more affable one.*)

(*We hear the sound of dogs barking, on occasion.*)

(*They watch.*)

MARK. *(eventually, out)* I hope it's alright that we're here.

PAULA. They don't care, Mark.

MARK. *(out)* I hope you don't mind if we…watch?

PAULA. You don't have to ask permission.

MARK. Well, I don't want them to think it's *strange*.

PAULA. It's a park; it's a public park.

MARK. It's a dog park, Paula.

PAULA. So?

MARK. We don't have one. *(out)* Not right now, anyway.

PAULA. We *did*.

MARK. *(out)* We've had many dogs.

PAULA. Many, many –

MARK. Labs, spaniels, dauschen –

PAULA. They all die; they're all dead.

MARK. …Paula.

PAULA. What, they do; they are.

MARK. *(out)* It's…true.

PAULA. *(a bit morbid)* We've killed them all, one by one.

MARK. Alright.

> *(out)*
>
> We've had many pets.
>
> (*They watch.*)

MARK. *(out)* Anyway, we're not exactly strangers to this place. We used to bring our…our animals here.

PAULA. We've had others.

MARK. Other kinds of pets.

PAULA. We killed them too.

MARK. Not on purpose, Paula. God, you make it sound – *(out)* We're not very good with animals. Which is to say, we're not...*bad.* They just...die on us a lot. Birds, gerbils, cats, lizards, they all die. Early. We have a pet cemetary in our backyard, to prove it. It's very large – very extensive, I'm afraid.

PAULA. There's a whole genus of rabbit buried out there.

MARK. We don't know that for certain, of course, but we've...run out, it seems. Of rabbit.

(They watch.)

PAULA. I miss the rabbits.

MARK. Yes, they were...fun.

PAULA. And the gerbils.

MARK. We did best with furry things.

PAULA. We did.

MARK. We've always been moderately good with land animals.

PAULA. Ugh, the *birds* were the worst.

MARK. Were they?

PAULA. Those were *your* idea.

MARK. I don't recall –

PAULA. I hate birds, actually.

MARK. You do not.

PAULA. I realized this. Pigeons, parrots, bats –

MARK. We never had *bats.*

PAULA. Surprisingly.

MARK. Bats aren't birds; they're rodents.

PAULA. *(a shudder)* Rats with wings.

MARK. Whatever, anyway –

PAULA. I hate them: noisy, smelly things.

MARK. *(out)* Our birds sang.

PAULA. Yes, they sang – terrible atonal songs, most of them – and they shat, mid flight, with precision…

MARK. She's been shat on; frequently. You've been shat on a lot.

PAULA. And then…they die.

MARK. Well, everything –

PAULA. They plummet. From those little perches and crash to the bottom of the cage.

MARK. It's sad, really.

PAULA. But I hated them, so…it was less –

MARK. *(out)* She doesn't mean that. We like all pets.

(They watch.)

PAULA. *(a shrug)* I liked the fish.

MARK. Yes, the fish!

PAULA. Fish are quiet; fish are simple.

MARK. I'd forgotten about the fish.

PAULA. Fish you can just flush down the toilet. Down the drain.

MARK. *(out)* We've flushed many.

PAULA. You can't flush a dog or a cat down the toilet. They don't make them big enough.

MARK. That's…true.

PAULA. The toilets, I mean.

MARK. *(out)* Anyway, whenever we lose one – well, anything really – we like to come here and just…sit.

PAULA. Mourn; grieve.

MARK. Paula. *(out) Talk,* she means. We like to be around other animals.

PAULA. *(some envy there)* The living.

MARK. So: I hope that's alright.

(They watch.)

MARK. We started all of this because we read somewhere –

PAULA. Mark.

MARK. They should know, Paula. *(out)* We started it all because we read somewhere – in a book?

PAULA. Some online thing.

MARK. Yes, we read that it's good to...ready one's self. For children?

PAULA. Ha.

MARK. That it instills a sense of responsibility. To...look after something. To take *care* of.

PAULA. *(conceding)* We did.

MARK. You've heard of this, I'm sure. So, we started buying pets. Small ones.

PAULA. The fish, the gerbils –

MARK. Yes.

PAULA. They died.

MARK. Yes.

PAULA. You've *told* them this already.

MARK. *Yes,* but they have short life-spans; they die anyway – neither are expected to live for very *long,* so...

PAULA. Little did we know.

MARK. So we got bigger one's.

PAULA. The birds, the beasts –

MARK. Yes, right. You'd be surprised how many kinds of pets are out there, really.

(They watch.)

PAULA. We almost got a donkey.

MARK. I wanted a donkey.

PAULA. But the laws; the danger of the thing.

MARK. Those things can kill you; one kick.

PAULA. We deserve to be killed.

MARK. We do *not. (out)* Anyway, those died too – even faster, it seemed. So we started to wonder...

PAULA. *You* did; I already knew.

MARK. We started to *worry:* was there some kind of...correlation here?

PAULA. There always is.

MARK. We'd been…trying, you see – all the while – and, well: nothing.

PAULA. …nothing.

MARK. We went to the doctor; got tested.

PAULA. Do we have to *tell* them this?

MARK. They should *know*, Paula. *(out)* We took the tests: Turns out my…whatever, is fine; I'm operational. Not that that's… But Paula is –

PAULA. I am…incapable, it seems.

MARK. We can't have children, you see?

PAULA. They get it, Mark.

MARK. And the books – the online thing – well, it doesn't ready you for that.

PAULA. No.

MARK. They don't have a chapter on that.

PAULA. *(morbid chuckle)* What: death?

MARK. They don't tell you what to do, if it doesn't *work*, you know?

PAULA. No, they don't.

MARK. And suddenly: all these poor animals, that we've –

PAULA. All that death.

MARK. For *nothing*, it seemed. And we were, well, upset. As you might imagine. So we got more –

PAULA. Any kind; whatever they had.

MARK. Anyone who would *sell* –

PAULA. We change pet stores a lot.

MARK. As a sort of…replacement, you see? As something to do?

PAULA. Ha.

MARK. But it hasn't been…Well, it's just gotten worse.

PAULA. *(mock cheer)* Just when you thought –

MARK .They die so *fast* on us now.

PAULA. *(out)* I touched an iguana in a pet store once and killed it instantly.

MARK. *(out)* She shocked it. Scuffing her feet on the carpet. How could she have – ?

PAULA. I *killed* it, Mark.

MARK. We paid for it, of course.

PAULA. We bought a corpse. It's in the backyard.

MARK. But it almost seems now as if they deliberately-intentionally…

PAULA. They do themselves in.

MARK. We don't know that.

PAULA. Our pets kill themselves now.

MARK. We don't *know* that.

PAULA. *(a shrug)* Saves us the trouble.

MARK. It's almost as if they…can *sense* something. *(a beat)* Like this last one –

PAULA. Please don't.

MARK. This last one –

PAULA. Please, Mark.

MARK. This last one – it's nobody's fault, Paula – I can tell them. *(back out)* This last dog – it was a dog – one of those little poodles? You know the kind – a mix, I think. They mix everything now, don't they?

PAULA. *(sadly)* They…do.

MARK. It's quite remarkable, really. And this one, well: we were assured this was a resilient breed. A resilient mix. It's a new one, so no one knows for *sure,* but –

PAULA. *(genuine remorse)* He was just a puppy.

MARK. A new litter. Very little; very young. But he was wise. Almost philosophical, it seemed.

PAULA. …yes.

MARK. Dogs can be that way, somehow. More than other animals.

PAULA. *(can't bear it)* Oh, god.

MARK. Dogs are like people sometimes, I think. *(a beat)* Why, I remember, this time when we had to put my childhood dog down –

PAULA. *(some urgency there)* Mark.

MARK. – this was our family dog, when I was a kid –

PAULA. They don't need to *know* this.

MARK. It's *my* story.

PAULA. I hate this story.

MARK. *(a bit firm)* It...correlates. *(back out)* This was *long* before Paula and I had met. And anyway, I remember this time, one day, when we came home and found our family dog had *turned*. We came home and he was this...different dog – he had alzhiemers, or something. Dogs have such *people* problems now – this is what I mean: dementia, cancer, colitis. It's astounding.

PAULA. *(shaking her head)* Jesus.

MARK. Well, it's *true*. At any rate, he'd turned violent. Irrascible, too. He'd cuddle with you one minute, then corner you the next. It was like living with a monster. This sometime lovable little monster. And we'd decided: it was time. It had to be done. So we took him to the vet.

PAULA. *Please,* not this one? I hate this –

MARK. And wouldn't you know it? The second we got there: bam! He was our old dog again. He *knew*. He cowered, and cuddled, and shook. And I panicked: had we misjudged him? Was he ill at all? Or had he just... forgotten? He had Alzhiemer's, as I said. And none of us could decide whether we felt guilty or...betrayed, you know?

PAULA. *(soft beg)* Mark?

MARK. But the decision had been made; and we handed him over; gave them the leash, and said...goodbye, or whatever. And just before my dog was dragged off, howling and whimpering, he looked at me – like a person, would – as if to say: you'll regret this. It was astounding: you'll regret this. I'll make you *pay. (a beat)* It was the same way our last dog looked at us – our mixed poodle puppy – before leaping into the oven.

(PAULA shuts her eyes tight.)

MARK. *(cont.)* I've often wondered whether all this has been penance, actually, somehow, for that day.

(**PAULA** *looks offstage, sadly, at the dogs.*)

But then – and this is what I'm *really* getting it – then, as we turn to leave: I see this little old woman with *her* dog. Some mutt – who knows what kind of dog this is – and the woman is crying. She's seen what's happened, of course, and she's *upset*. Very upset. And so I get upset; *I* start crying, because now there's this witness, this…audience, to the whole thing. *(A bit for Paula.)* Which is important, I think. To have someone there. Someone to *share* these things with. *(Back out.)* So we cry, all of us – and it's terrible.

(**PAULA** *sits up, suddenly.*)

But then her dog – the mutt – it leaps out of her lap and just licks me. Kisses, all over my face. It comforts me. It somehow knows too! Only it understands the human *complexity* of this situation, you see? And it's… forgiven me.

(**PAULA** *rises.*)

Here's this little old lady, balling for someone else's animal, balling her eyes out, but this little mutt *knew!* Amazing!

(**PAULA** *walks offstage.*)

They say animals can feel profound emotion. Wolves howl at the moon; lobsters mate for life…

(We hear the sound of dogs barking wildly…)

I've heard of dogs who – when they know their going to die? – who'll crawl under the porch to be alone. Whales, who'll beach themselves to spare the sea.

(We hear the sound of dogs growling now…)

MARK *(cont.)* And I have to say, I respect that…that under-standing. Of life; or, of one's, well…self?

(We hear sound of some concerned voices, too…)

Because, sometimes...sometimes I think the loneliest animal on earth...is us.

(...then the sound of something being savagely ripped apart.)

(eventually, having just noticed she's gone) Paula?

(lights out)

THE GRAVE

by Gabe McKinley

CHARACTERS

THE MAN - 40s or 50s
NICK - 30s

ABOUT THE PRODUCTION

THE GRAVE had its world premiere in July 2008 at the Lake George Theater Lab. The prodcution was directed by Rosemary Andress and was designed by Shoko Kambara.

MAN . . . . Jose Febus
NICK . . . . Drew Cortese

THE GRAVE had its New York premiere at the Peter Jay Sharp Theater in July 2008 as part of The Samuel French Off Off Broadway Festival of Short Plays. The production was produced by Shoot First Theater, directed by Andy Goldberg and designed by Shoko Kambara.

MAN . . . . Neil Magnuson
NICK . . . . Gabriel Silva

ABOUT THE AUTHOR

Gabe McKinley's plays include *The Kitchen Sink Play* (Lake George Theater Lab), *Love Sick* (NY Fringe), *Welcome Home Rock Rogers* (NY Fringe) and *Funny*. Mr. McKinley is currently studying playwriting with Christopher Shinn in The New School for Drama's masters program.

(Lights raise to half light, the light reveals a remote nat-ural landscape, an out of the way place, one far from peering eyes. Sitting on a rock, lantern at his side, is the MAN. The MAN is wearing a suit with the jacket off to reveal a shoulder holster with a gun in it. The MAN smokes and continues to constantly smoke throughout the scene – one cigarette after another. Nearby, NICK digs a hole – a grave – in which he is ankle deep. NICK is in suit pants and a button down – not dressed for the task at hand. There is a long stretch of silence, during which the MAN smokes and NICK digs and sweats. Finally, NICK takes a moment and wipes his brow with his sleeve.)

NICK. This is not how I'd hoped this day would turn out.

(beat)

You don't talk much.

(beat)

You don't mind if I talk, do you?
Talky?
You. Me. Talky?

(beat)

What's the matter? Is it because they made you work on the weekend?

(beat)

Could be worse. Look at me. It could be worse.

*(**NICK** goes back to digging. He continues to dig the grave on and off – deeper and deeper – the remainder of the scene.)*

I don't know what I'm complaining about. I'm out-side. Fresh air. Working with my hands. It's just like camp – except I got to come home from camp. *(beat)*

It's a joke. I joke when I am...let's say uncomfortable. I think uncomfortable is the right word for how I'm feeling right now. Do you know any good jokes? *(beat)* We have never been truly introduced. My name is Nicholas Beck, I should say Dr. Nicholas Beck. My parents spent a lot of money on that first part, the doctor part, can't forget the doctor part. *(beat)* I'm a veterinarian. The good doctor. Maybe not good... Did they tell you that? Did they tell you anything? Yep. A Vet. Since I was a little kid that was all I ever wanted to be – and I got to be one. Most kids never grow up to be what they want to be. I guess if they did you'd see a hell of a lot more wizards and ninjas walking the streets. I was just lucky or some... *(beat)* I went to the University of Pennsylvania School of Veterinary Medicine. I have loved animals my whole life. *(beat)* What's that you ask? My favorite? My favorite animal is Equus Calallus. What's that you ask? It's Latin. Oh, you meant what's it mean? It's Latin for horse. There is nothing more beautiful on this planet than a horse, in my humble opinion. And a thoroughbred? A thoroughbred pony is...is simply beyond words. People say a lot of things are beautiful in this world – ya know? Paintings, sculptures, women and...money. Especially money. But nothing is as stunning as a thoroughbred pony in motion. God got it right that time. He nailed it. He threw a hard eight. God deserved a day off after that. He earned it. *(beat)* Not that I don't like women. I love women, but even the most gorgeous women in the world would be hard pressed to keep up with what you find at Belmont most days. *(beat)* Don't say anything to my wife, okeydokey? That is between you, me and this hole. *(beat)* Strong silent type. *(beat)* You have a wife? I do. No kids though. *(beat)* You are quite a conversationalist. *(beat)* Yeah horses, that is why I work out at the track. I couldn't get enough of being around those beautiful animals. Most of the people I went to school with either joined a practice or started their own. I tried that for a little while – I worked with this old cus Doc McRae. But I got sick of giving rabies shots and spaying kittens. I was a railbird – I'd spend most of my time out at the Woodlands anyway – as a result I met a lot of trainers and owners. Pretty soon I started looking after their stables. One trainer tells another trainer tells another owner, you know how it is? *(beat)* Maybe you don't. Not in your line of work. Am I boring you? *(beat)* No answers? *(laughing to himself)* I feel like I am talking to myself here. But I'm not, am I? *(beat)* Look at least give me a cigarette if you're not going to talk to me.

(The **MAN** *takes a beat – then slowly removes a cigarette from his pack – and slowly lights it – then hands it to* **NICK.** *)*

It lives. Thank you. I tell you, it was perfect, working at the track that is. I got to spend the whole day looking after all these amazing animals. "Salad days" right? "…My salad days, When I was green in judgment, cold in blood…" *(beat)* You know what that's from? Three guesses. *(beat)* No. No. No. It's Shakespeare. Cleopatra. I'm not as pretty as Elizabeth Taylor, but ah…*(beat)* Yeah, so, it was a good time working at the track. I'd go out there and make sure the horses were sound. Most of the injuries were…are…pretty common – bleeding – colic – bucked shins – bowed tendons – normal stuff. Course it wasn't always great times. Every once in a while I'd have to put down a horse. That was always so hard. I mean you have this beautiful animal that is designed to run – touched by God to run and that is all it wants to do – and then it zigs when it should've zagged – comes down funny on its ankle or knee or just gets spooked and crashes into something – and it's over. So amazingly strong and athletic and totally fragile at the same time. I never understood that…I never understood how a horse could be so powerful and then crumble like that – like a sugar cube when it gets wet. *(beat)* Couple of times I had to euthanize a horse on the track. It was terrible – You're looking in its eyes – looking into a horses eyes is like looking into God's eyes – it's so scared...it just knows that something isn't right. *(beat)* The first time I ever had to put a horse down at the track – it was this gray mare called Fortune Teller – she shattered her leg at the mile marker. I am about to shoot her up with the drug – Sodium Pento-barbital – and the horse is staring at me, and I swear to God it just knows what is going to happen – and I want to make it feel at ease – I thought I should say a prayer – but I couldn't remember any – so, out of nowhere, I start to recite that nursery rhyme "Ride a Cock Horse to Banbury Cross." I don't know where it came from – I hadn't heard the thing in years. But there I am hold-ing this animal's head, staring it in the eyes with tears running down my face and I'm singing "Ride a cock horse to Banbury Cross / To see a fine lady upon a white horse / With rings on her fingers and bells on her toes / She shall have music wherever she goes." You know that one? I always liked that one – I always thought it'd be nice to have music wherever I went. I just kept saying it over and over again until it was done. I just wanted the horse to know it was not alone. You understand? No one should be alone when they go... *(beat)* Horses don't shut their eyes when you kill them – did you know that? *(beat)* I got an idea. Why don't we just finish this tomorrow? Knock off early – grab a couple of beers. Whaddya say?

(NICK steps out of the hole. The MAN stands up. They stare at one another. NICK quickly gets back to work.)

For some reason I feel like I can talk to you. *(beat)* Con-fession time. Just like when I was a kid. *(beat)* Forgive me father for I have sinned. It has been many years since my last confession, and I have done many bad things. I started helping rig races for your employer a few years ago, just for the extra cash. He needed some-one to fix a race here and there – and I was able to help him. As long as whatever I did to the animal didn't permanently hurt the horse – I thought why not make some cash? I must have fixed a hundred races over the years. You'd think I'd be rich. I mean everybody at the track is making dirty money one way or another – why should I starve, right? I got debts. Let's just say, I've missed a few trifectas in my day. *(beat)* Slowing down a horse is pretty simple really. You don't have to use drugs if you are smart – just a piece of sponge in the nostril or a ping pong ball, anything to slow down the amount of air the animal was getting. Hell, I met one guy who gave his horse apples soaked in vodka whenever he wanted it to have an "off" race. Now speeding up a horse is a different story. Then it's better living through chemistry. Mostly you try to remove any pain the animal was living with and then get it a boost without getting caught. I didn't like it because the horse could break down easy if it was not feeling any pain. But like I said, the money is good. *(beat)* Big Fella? You wanna lend a hand here? It'll save you time. Look you take the shovel, I'll take the gun and ah…I guess that isn't fair is it? But, who said life is fair, huh? *(beat)* I mean you are going to have to fill this hole back in all by yourself, right? Look I'm sorry, this is just my first time in this situation. You know I could make a joke about it being my last, but you won't laugh. You won't even smile. Come on. What's your name, buddy?

(The MAN cracks a smile, an internal chuckle. It fades quickly. Silence.)

Thank you for that. No name, huh? I had an imaginary friend when I was kid named Cal. Can I call you Cal? *(beat)* The last thing I was doing to speed up horses – now this is genius – the last thing before all this went down, was to dope the horse with painkilling snake venom. I shit you not – from cobras – because there was no way in hell they were going to test for it. It sounds crazy but it worked. Then after the pain killer I'd give them this stuff called Epogen – that got more blood to the heart – increased endurance. I was pretty good at being a criminal veterinarian. I am really good. *(beat)* Are you good at what you do, Cal? Huh? I bet you're good at what you do. *(beat)* Look Cal, if you don't wanna talk to me – just say so. *(beat)* I almost got you there. I almost got you to say something. *(beat)* That's it. I'm sick of talking to you. I know you're listening. I am not going to say another word – not another fucking word. I am going finish this ditch – this grave – in silence.

*(**NICK** continues to dig in silence for a short time.)*

You know why I'm here, Cal? Why every time you see a pony run you're gonna think of me out here? Because… I wouldn't kill an animal that didn't deserve to die. Need to die. I'm asking you to understand that. *(beat)* Taking life. *(beat)* I don't think I need to explain what that is like to you, do I? *(beat)* I was asked to kill a healthy horse by the people you work for. Horse was named Needle's Eye. A beautiful horse – the most beautiful horse I ever saw. A horse that broke your heart every time you saw it run – because there was no way anything was ever going to be that wonderful… that exquisite… I'm a dirty veterinarian, but I am not a killer of… Shouldn't that get me something? Maybe not a place in heaven – but something? They said it was easy to make it look like an accident. They said I am the only one – and who would suspect the good doctor? Not you, right? Kill God's greatest moment – his masterpiece…for insurance money. They say do it or else. Or else what?

*(**NICK** looks around at his situation.)*

This. Or else this.

(silence)

I said no.

(silence)

I can keep digging all the way to China if you want. You know in China – in the labor camps – when they execute somebody they make the family of the guy they just shot, pay for the bullet they used to kill him? Are you going to make me pay for this shovel, Cal?

(**NICK** *steps out of the hole. The* **MAN** *stands up, places his hand on his holster. They stare at each other for a moment.*)

I'm almost done with this hole, and I have to ask you something. I want you to think about this. Think about it hard. I want to ask you to let me walk into those bushes over there and just keep walking…I feel like we have an understanding, you and me. *(beat)* I'm just an animal doctor that didn't want to kill…You've been listening. You know what…I have a wife and she likes me above ground. Come on my friend. My friend. Look at me. Please. Look me in the eye like one animal to another. Look me in the eye – and tell me I deserve to die. You can't…

(**NICK** *walks slowly toward the* **MAN**.)

Look me in the eye. I'm a man just like you. Look me in the eye please. Look me in the eye like…

(*The* **MAN** *grabs* **NICK** *by the throat and throws him to the ground like a sack of potatoes. The* **MAN** *takes a cowering* **NICK** *by the scruff of the neck and pulls him to his knees at the edge of the grave.*)

What do I do? What do I do now? Please… My voice can't be the last one I ever hear. I need an answer. I need to know I'm not…alone! Please say something… please tell me what to do…. please…

(*silence*)

Please.

(*beat*)

MAN. Close your eyes.

(*beat*)

NICK. Thank you.

(*Beat.* **NICK***, hot tears running down his face, begins to recite the rhyme "Ride a Cock Horse to Banbury Cross." During the second time through, the* **MAN** *recites it with him.*)

NICK. Ride a cock horse to Banbury Cross
 To see a fine lady upon a white horse
 With rings on her fingers and bells on her toes
 She shall have music wherever she goes.

NICK.	**MAN.**
Ride a cock horse to Banbury Cross	Ride a cock horse to Banbury Cross
To see a fine lady upon a white horse	To see a fine lady upon a white horse
With rings on her fingers	With rings on her fingers
and bells on her toes	and bells on her toes
She shall have music...	She shall have music...

(The **MAN** *lowers his pistol to the back of* **NICK***'s head.)*
(Slow fade to black out.)

JUNIPER; JUBILEE

by Janine Nabers

CHARACTERS

JUNIPER: A Black South African. Early Teens. Once a Sudanese orphan.

CARL: An Afrikaner. 40s. A Médecins Sans Frontières. Juniper's adopted father.

DEENA: A White American. 40s. Juniper's adopted mother.

MATT: A Jewish American. Early Teens. Wears a yarmulke throughout the play.

DOCTOR: A White American female. Young. Blonde.

CHORUS: African women. Juniper's fear manifested in sound and dance.

AUTHOR'S NOTES

/ Indicates when the next actor begins speaking.

All off stage sound effects are actor generated. For information regarding the original music used in the Festival production please contact Giorgos Kolias at www.georgekolias.com.
.
All Arabic text has been transliterated.

ABOUT THE PRODUCTION

JUNIPER; JUBILEE was first performed April 24th - 26, 2008 at The New School for Drama Random Act festival. The cast and crew included the following people:

JUNIPER	Brittany Bellizeare
CARL	Mark Cajigao
DEENA	Rena Krumholz
MATT	Ben Schnickel
DOCTOR	Grace Evans
CHORUS	Mia Kristin Smith, LaChrisha Brown, Ayo Cummings

Director: Alexandra Hastings
Dialect Coach: Patricia Fletcher
Composer: George Kolias

The 33rd Annual Samuel French Off Off Broadway Short Play Festival production of this play included the following people:

JUNIPER . . . . Brittany Bellizeare
CARL . . . . Andreas C. Tselepos
DEENA . . . . .Rena Krumholz
MATT . . . . Ben Schnickel
DOCTOR . . . . .Grace Evans
CHORUS . . . . Mia Kristin Smith, LaChrisha Brown, Ayo Cummings

Director: Alexandra Hastings
Dialect Coach: Patricia Fletcher
Composer: George Kolias
Stage Manager: David Hastings

ABOUT THE AUTHOR

Janine Nabers had her first play produced at 19. She is an alumna of the National Theater Institute. She has a BA in Drama and MFA in playwriting. She is 25.

JUNIPER; JUBILEE was written under the guidance of
Christopher Shinn.
It is dedicated to my parents and Gina Leon.

*(Lights rise on **JUNIPER** who sits on the ground and writes in her journal.)*

*(Behind her at a distance we see her parents, **CARL** and **DEENA**. They sort through moving boxes – an occasional eye on their daughter.)*

JUNIPER. – and where is the *water*? Everywhere I look I see concrete and Astroturf. I sit on it and I don't like it. This *fake* grass. It makes my skin itch.

(She stops writing and closes her eyes.)

I close my eyes and try to imagine: South Africa. Umbrella thorns and Impala's. The Orange River stretched out for miles. And then I open my eyes...

(She does, examining a house and neighborhood we do not see.)

and I see *Jeep Cherokee's!*

(She goes back to writing in her journal.)

DEENA. Do you think she likes it?

CARL. No.

*(**CARL** and **DEENA** disappear into the house.)*

JUNIPER. – this city is too gray! When the sun is out? Gray. Only a little *less gray.* American flags hanging on every porch. Too many to count: Red. White. Blue and gray –

*(A boy on roller blades breezes onto the street where **JUNIPER** is. This is **MATT**. In his back pocket are drumsticks. He notices **JUNIPER** and circles around her playfully. They lock eyes right as he disappears. **JUNIPER** goes back to writing in her journal as **DEENA** and **CARL** re-emerge from the house to gather more boxes.)*

DEENA. So you'll have the talk with her before/ you

CARL. Yes. Of course. I'll talk to/ her.

JUNIPER. And then there's this house. White wood. White fence. It *breathes*, this house it does. The air conditioning comes on, and the entire place shifts, like its taking a deep breath in and then /exhaling

DEENA. Juniper.

(**JUNIPER** *stops writing.*)

Come on it's getting late. Bring your boxes inside.

(*nothing*)

I get it. You're still mad at us for moving here. But you can be mad, inside. Okay?

(**JUNIPER** *finally turns to look at her mother: A stare off.* **DEENA** *has gotten good at it.*)

Fine. If you're going to stand there and pout, fine, Juniper. *Pout.* But you will help with the unpacking of this house. Is that –

JUNIPER. *Okay.*

(**DEENA** *picks up a box and takes it into the house.*)

JUNIPER. I *hate* it here. I hate this house.

(**MATT** *breezes by again. This time a little more coolly – his focus completely on* **JUNIPER**. *He circles around her again and again. She giggles.*)

(**CARL** *comes out of the house and catches the two of them.* **MATT** *scurries off.*)

CARL. Juniper.

(**JUNIPER** *sees her father and then turns away from him.*)

It's not so bad, is it?

(**JUNIPER** *remains unmoved.* **CARL** *moves closer towards her. He has something behind his back.*)

I have something for you.

(*She looks at him and slightly smiles.*)

Go on.

(*She closes her eyes and holds out her hands.* **DEENA** *appears outside of the house – watching from a distance.*

CARL *reveals a small shrub.* **JUNIPER** *opens her eyes.)*

CARL. *(cont.)* Do you know what it is? It's a healing shrub. A Juniper tree. Its oil is used as a medicine to rid people of pain. Now you'll have a piece of Africa with you here in America.

(He is gentle from a distance.)

You know the first time we held you, you smelled of Juniper and Sage. Your body was so tiny. So weak... but you had this *voice.* This jubilant sound. Look at you now...look at you now. You're beautiful.

(A moment. **CARL** *turns away from* **JUNIPER**.*)*

JUNIPER. Dad?

(He smiles.)

CARL. Okay. Tell me. What do you miss most? On the count of three...one...two...

JUNIPER/CARL. *Boerewors.*

(They laugh.)

JUNIPER. Eating it until I'm so full I can't even blink. Summer. The barbeques. Lying on sun burnt grass all day long!

CARL. My favorite time of year.

JUNIPER. The checkered tiles on the kitchen floor. The pit pat of your shoes against the surface. That's how I could always tell you came back. I think I miss that sound the most.

(beat)

I can always tell you've been assigned a mission. You plant things around the yard.

Where are you going this time?

CARL. Njamena. Chad. I leave at the beginning of your school term. I'll be back in March.

JUNIPER. Take me with you.

CARL. You know that's not possible. I promise to write. Every second I get. Every –

(JUNIPER sets the shrub down and walks away from CARL.)

Sweetheart, look at me.

(She doesn't. CARL glances at DEENA who continues to stand in the distance.)

Juniper? How are you feeling today? Have you been in any pain?

(JUNIPER is still unmoved.)

Your mother and I talked about you seeing a *specialist* here...now that you're – getting older. You're body is changing. You'll have someone to talk to.
Juniper?

(Nothing. CARL picks up the shrub.)

They never grow in straight, these trees. No matter where they lie their limbs are always twisted /always...

JUNIPER. Dad.

(A moment.)

Are you okay?

CARL. Our leaving South Africa was for the best. America is...*safe*. We live here now, but you and I will always be Afrikaans.

(JUNIPER hugs her father. She clings to him.)

JUNIPER. The stars in America are so *small*. Why is that? And the air...if I sit outside too long...the smell makes my head hurt. Everything in this city moves so fast and then there are the sounds. I miss red rocky roads and crickets that sing like talking moons. Even when I close my eyes and think of Africa *with all my might*... even then I hear so much *noise*.
I hate it here. I *hate* this house.

(DEENA disappears into the house. CARL rocks June as she melts into him. He sings to her.)

CARL. Juna ba-la-la long cuckoo
Juna ba-la-la long tweh tweh

Juna ba-la-la long cuckoo
Juna ba-la-la long tweh tweh.

(**CARL** *kisses* **JUNIPER**.)

I'll be back soon.

(*Lights shift as* **DEENA** *brings out* **CARL**'s *travel bag and coat.* **JUNIPER** *watches as her parents say goodbye to one another.*)

DEENA. Be careful.

CARL. I'll call you when I land.

(*Both women watch* **CARL** *exit. After a moment* **DEENA** *hands* **JUNIPER** *her backpack.*)

DEENA. June – hurry up. You don't want to miss the bus.

(*Lights shift as* **JUNIPER** *appears in front of the school bus stop.* **DEENA** *stands next to her. Neither one of them look at each other.*)

DEENA. You know I'm not crazy about this place, either. I grew up in this country and I never liked it. It always made me feel so anxious. Like I had to keep moving – running? It was impossible for me to stay still. I think I started taking pictures so I could capture it – *stillness.* See what I was missing. So I made it my job. Saw the world. Ended up in Sudan. And then I met your father and we had you...we made a home in South Africa. And I *stopped* running.

(**DEENA** *examines her daughter.*)

Is that a pimple on your face?

(**JUNIPER** *is ruined.*)

Oh don't worry, Sweetheart. You're starting to break out. It's okay. We can fix it.
It's just – you're starting to get so big – so gorgeous.

(*Sound of a rattling African instrument can be heard from off.*)

(**JUNIPER** *is struck with pain in her pelvis.* **DEENA** *sees this.*)

DEENA. Juniper?

JUNIPER. I'm/ fine.

DEENA. Honey/are you

JUNIPER. I said: *I'm fine.*

(A moment.)

DEENA. You're fine.

*(**DEENA** examines her daughter. She wants to touch her, but doesn't.)*

You know the first time we held you – you smelled of Juniper and sage.

Your body was so tiny. So weak…but you had this *voice.* This jubilant sound/ and

DEENA/JUNIPER. "Look at you now…look at you now…"

*(**DEENA** trails off as **JUNIPER** mocks her mother. The school bell rings. **JUNIPER** grabs her stuff and runs off. **DEENA** realizes she's still holding **JUNIPER**'s lunch.)*

DEENA. Oh Juniper! June bug! You forgot your –

(She is gone.)

Lunch. *Shit.*

*(Lights shift as **DEENA** exits and a second bell rings. **MATT** walks toward his locker. He carries drumsticks. **JUNIPER** sees him. He looks up as she walks away.)*

MATT. Wait – hey, I know you.

(She stops.)

You live on my block. Wood Creek?

(She turns and nods.)

We're *neighbors.*

(He giggles as he drums on his locker.)

Well, kinda. I live across the street from you. You moved in late summer, right?

*(African drum echoes. **JUNIPER** is in pain.)*

Are you okay?

(A moment. She nods.)

'Kay...Where are you from?

(Sounds of a group of kids making fun of **MATT** *and* **JUNIPER** *from offstage. They call him "jew-tard" and make monkey noises at her. We do not see any of them.)*

(It gets louder.)

JUNIPER. Why?

MATT. What? – Oh. no, uh, reason. I was just, you know like – SHUT UP – making conversation.

(He turns around. A sign on his back reading: "Loser" is now seen. **JUNIPER** *points it out. He rips it apart.)*

I'm *totally* okay. Go on.

JUNIPER. I grew up in South Africa.

MATT. No way! Really?

JUNIPER. You've been?

MATT. Nah, but I think Nelson Mandela's pretty dope.

(He makes a black power fist. **JUNIPER** *looks at her feet.)*

So that blonde lady that you live with is your Mom, right? She's your Mom?

JUNIPER. I was *adopted* when I was three. From Sudan. In case you're wondering –

(He begins to drum again. The sound of an African drum creeps in once more and begins to build. **JUNIPER** *begins to pulse)*

MATT. In case *you're* wondering, I'm in a *band*. I practice all the time. School mostly – cause it *sucks*. The only time I put my sticks down is when I'm in the bathroom – like on the toilet or in the shower. Even when I eat I have a stick in my hand. It drives my mom crazy. Which is *awesome*....

*(***JUNIPER** *stumbles.)*

MATT. Are you – hey – ?

(He supports her.)

You okay?

*(**JUNIPER** regains her strength.)*

JUNIPER. A bug. I have a bug.

MATT. That *sucks*. I hate being sick. It's the smell of it, mostly. You lie in bed for hours drinking the same stuff until you can't even taste the difference between soup or water, or *juice*… and when you get the energy to get up and walk around – I don't know it's the smell – that yucky zombie like smell? Even if I shower like ten times in one day it just sits with me. But when it's gone, the smell…at least I can breathe in actual *clean air*. That's when I know I'm finally okay.

I hope you feel better soon.

(She examines him.)

JUNIPER. Will you walk me home?

(He smiles.)

MATT. 'Kay.

*(They walk halfway around the stage. **MATT** stops suddenly and takes **JUNIPER**'s book bag and binder.)*

I'm Matt.

JUNIPER. Juniper.

*(**MATT** holds her binder, drumming on it as they walk the second half of the stage. They are drawn to each other – they move in closer. Lights shift slightly.)*

MATT. I've never been to Africa but I've always wanted to go /there

JUNIPER. You should. You really /should

MATT. Not like just one country but the entire continent. Maybe when I go you can come. I mean with me. That be really great.

JUNIPER. If we go – you have to start by seeing the waterfalls in Zimbabwe –

MATT. Waterfalls?

JUNIPER. The biggest in the world. A mile long – Or the Roman ruins in Libya! My dad took me one summer. It was – ! And *Mozambique*. The safaris! You'd die the sight /is so

MATT. I can't/ wait!

JUNIPER. *Beautiful.*

(*beat*)

Do you like living here?

MATT. I've never been anywhere else.

(*pause*)

No.

JUNIPER. If I were a bird, I'd fly back home and cut my wings. And even if I *bled* at least I'd be there.

MATT. Juniper?

(**MATT** *takes a step closer to* **JUNIPER**. *She takes a setp back.*)

JUNIPER. I don't normally –

MATT. It's okay.

(*She points towards his sticks.*)

JUNIPER. You can put them down if you want.

(*He does.*)

And you can –

(*She puts his hands on her hips.*)

MATT. 'Kay.

(*They kiss slowly. After a moment* **DEENA** *immerges from the house. She is barefoot and wearing* **CARL**'s *shirt.*)

DEENA. Juniper!

(*They pull away from each other.*)

MATT. Good evening Mrs…um…

(**JUNIPER** *whispers.*)

JUNIPER. *Mason.*

MATT. 'Kay.

>*(He waves.)*

>Mrs. Mason. I'm Matthew? Benkendorf. Juniper's Boy-friend.

>*(**JUNIPER** wants to die.)*

>We go to school together. I live across the street.

>*(**DEENA** looks across the way.)*

DEENA. The house with the American flag?

>*(He nods.)*

>I see. Juniper. Go inside.

JUNIPER. But –

DEENA. *Now.*

>*(**JUNIPER** looks at **MATT** and then exits. **MATT** stands up straight.)*

MATT. Is Mr. Mason home? I'd like to ask him a question. Man to man.

DEENA. Mr. Mason is not home and no you cannot date my daughter.

>Matthew Benkendorf, is it? Stay away from Juniper.

>*(**DEENA** shuts the door as lights shift to **JUNIPER** on the other side.)*

>*(They are in mid argument)*

JUNIPER. You're not being fair!

DEENA. You are not allowed to see that boy.

JUNIPER. He's the only thing about this place that I like! He's my *friend* –

DEENA. Juniper, he *is not* your *friend*. You don't do things like that with your friends –

>You have to listen to me, okay? Seeing him isn't saf –

>You're too young.

JUNIPER. *Seeing him isn't what?*

>*(beat)*

DEENA. Sit down.

>*(**JUNIPER** sits.)*

DEENA. The day we moved in – I realized that you had started your period. You've been hiding it from me for weeks. Why?

(**JUNIPER** *doesn't look at her mother.*)

Before your father left we discussed you seeing a professional who – If you have questions about what happened to you when you were a baby, we can talk/ about it

JUNIPER. We've never been able talk about it.

DEENA. Seeing him isn't *safe.* I'm trying to protect you.

(*beat*)

June bug. Don't shut me out – I'm *here*, okay. We can talk to each other so we can figure out a /way to

JUNIPER. I don't want to figure anything out. Not by you. Not by Doctors. Not by anyone. I just want to be left alone!

(**JUNIPER** *hurries off.*)

DEENA. June Bug.

(**DEENA** *exits as lights slowly rise on a sleeping* **JUNIPER** *in the middle of the night.*)

(*After a moment a distorted rhythm is heard from off. Followed by* **CARL** *and* **DEENA***'s voices echoing: "You know the first time we held you, you smelled of* **JUNIPER** *and sage…[and so on]")*

(*The Rhythm builds as different voices are now heard. They speak in Arabic: "Lakad wa-fet dohree beeseefatee ka abak," [I have fulfilled my role as your father] and "Jsmak hoo baladak" [Your body is your Country]*)

(**JUNIPER** *tosses in her sleep and then opens her eyes. She is overcome with pain between her legs. She looks through the sheets frantically until she finds something. She lifts it up into the light as the beating of the drums build.*)

(*It's a knife.* **JUNIPER** *screams.*)

(*A light comes on from somewhere off and we see* **DEENA** *sprinting in her night robe.*)

(**DEENA** *enters the room and turns the light on.*)

DEENA. Juniper!

(The sounds cease.)

(Lights shift to an open room with a sitting area for two. A woman wearing a blouse and dress pants opens the door as **JUNIPER** *enters with* **DEENA**.)*

DOCTOR. You must be Juniper. Hello. My name /is

JUNIPER. I can't stay long. I have school.

(The **DOCTOR** *smiles.)*

DOCTOR. That's what your mom said. This shouldn't take very long.

(**DEENA** *nods towards the* **DOCTOR** *and then exits.* **JUNIPER** *watches her go.*)

You can sit if you want.

(**JUNIPER** *does not move.*)

DOCTOR. Okay.

(The **DOCTOR** *gestures to her chair.)*

Do you mind if I – ?

(The **DOCTOR** *sits.)*

JUNIPER. You don't look like a Doctor.

DOCTOR. What do they look like?

(**JUNIPER** *shrugs and walks towards another part of the room.*)

(She examines the things around her.)

JUNIPER. Different I guess.

(The **DOCTOR** *pulls out a bag of candy.* **JUNIPER** *looks at the* **DOCTOR**.)*

DOCTOR. It's a bad habit of mine. I eat them throughout the day and sometimes by lunch – would you like one? Go ahead. Take as many as you want. Just not the red ones. They're my favorite.

JUNIPER. What if I like the red ones?

DOCTOR. Then I would share them with you.

(A moment.)

JUNIPER. I don't like M&Ms.

> **(JUNIPER** *continues to move around the room. She does not look at the* **DOCTOR.** *The* **DOCTOR** *watches her.)*

Is there any candy in particular that you do like?

JUNIPER. If I said the name you wouldn't know it. It's South African.

> *(The Doctor is still.* **JUNIPER** *finally looks at her.)*

They're called Holley Molleys.

> *(A single beat of a drum.* **JUNIPER** *turns her head to see where it came from.)*

DOCTOR. What do you like about them?

> *(Another drum beat:* **JUNIPER** *closes her eyes.)*

JUNIPER. If I were a bird –

> *(More beating of the drum.* **JUNIPER** *covers her ears.)*

DOCTOR. Juniper –

JUNIPER. I'd fly back home and cut /my wings

DOCTOR. Can you open your eyes and look at me?

> *(The* **DOCTOR** *puts her hands on* **JUNIPER***'s – a gentle struggle until she opens her eyes. The sound stops.* **JUNI-PER** *turns to run away.)*

DOCTOR. Juniper, wait!

> *(She stops.)*

I've never had Holley Molleys, but I would like to try them. Next time, if you decide to come back and visit me. We can sit here and eat them. Anything you want.

(beat.)

Until then...

> *(The* **DOCTOR** *turns to retrieve a pad of paper and pen as an African woman wearing a tribal gown emerges out of the shadows and into the* **DOCTORS** *office. She reaches for* **JUNIPER.***)*

(JUNIPER *gasps and runs out the door. The* DOCTOR *turns and examines the empty room.*)

(Lights shift as JUNIPER *appears under a streetlight. She faces an unlit house and calls out.)*

JUNIPER. Matt!

(MATT *appears up above.*)

MATT. Juniper!

(They whisper.)

What are you doing here?

JUNIPER. I had to get out of that house!

MATT. I tried to call you. But your mom –

JUNIPER. I know.

(slight pause)

MATT. Hey, June?

JUNIPER. Hey what.

MATT. I couldn't stop thinking about you.

JUNIPER. Matt. If we ran away tonight. Would you take me somewhere far away from here.

MATT. Yeah. I'll take you wherever you want to go.

JUNIPER. Somewhere safe.

(We hear whispers from off: "La takhafee" [Don't be scared]. JUNIPER *looks around.)*

Away from the strange people and noises.

MATT. Juniper?

(JUNIPER *is in pain.*)

MATT. Are you okay?

Look. There's one place that I go sometimes. To play drums. It's this abandoned house. I can take you there…if you want.

(She nods.)

Okay.

(MATT *disappears into the house. Light's slowly shift as*

he comes out of his house with a flash light. They soon enter a dilapidated house.)

Watch your step.

(They go inside.)

Kinda weird huh?

(Whispers from off: Cuhlshe Zayn Ya Saghiratee [It's okay, little one])

JUNIPER. What's that noise?

MATT. What?

(He takes off his jacket and puts it around her.)

Oh that? I don't know. Some people say this place is haunted. But we'll be okay. I have a black belt in Karate.

(He sets the flashlight down. They are lit romantically in the darkness.)

MATT. Hey June?

JUNIPER. Hey what?

MATT. I wrote you a song. I mean it's not *done* yet. And it doesn't have a title. And I don't have the words, really? *But.* I have the beat. You see the beat – the *rhythm?* Is me. And the words that fall into it – well, they're you, but I haven't really figured/ out

JUNIPER. Matt?

MATT. Yeah.

JUNIPER. Kiss me.

*(**MATT** drops his drumsticks and they make out.)*

MATT. Can I touch you?

JUNIPER. Uh-huh.

*(They make out more. **MATT** and **JUNIPER** are both breathing hard.)*

*(**JUNIPER** pulls away.)*

MATT. What?

JUNIPER. Nothing. It just.

(JUNIPER looks down at his crotch. MATT does as well.)

MATT. Yeah, I can't really help it. It does that.

(beat)

Is that okay?

JUNIPER. Yeah.

(JUNIPER pulls him towards her once more. They kiss. Drumming from off. It builds.)

Kiss me harder.

(He does. MATT comes up for air.)

MATT. Juniper?

(JUNIPER won't let him go. JUNIPER's body begins to pulse. Her arousal turns to pain.)

JUNIPER. Take the pain away.

MATT. What?

(MATT pulls away from JUNIPER. His lip is bleeding. The Arabic whispers are heard once more. JUNIPER gasps as she turns the flashlight off.)

(A moment. MATT speaks in darkness.)

MATT. Juniper? Why'd you turn the light out?

(MATT turns the flashlight on and points it at JUNIPER who is surrounded by a chorus of women in tribal African gowns. They dance around her in unison. JUNIPER's body sways to the music as if in a trance.)

(MATT does not see the women.)

MATT. Are you okay?

(MATT continues to stare at JUNIPER who moves more and more. They dance. Their faces filled with joy as they shout in ululation.)

MATT. Juniper...Are you O– I'm gonna go get your mom, okay? I'm gonna go get Mrs. Mason.

(MATT runs off stage as lights shift – Coming to full. The ritual continues – the music louder. The older African woman [first seen in the Doctor's office] breaks away

from the dance and pulls JUNIPER *towards her as the
other women restrain* JUNIPER*'s arms and spread her
legs. The women try to sooth* JUNIPER *as they chant:
La tak-hafee [Don't be scared]. The older woman then
removes a knife and holds it up to the sky in a dramatic
gesture and then strikes* JUNIPER *between her legs muti-
lating her.)*

(JUNIPER *wails.)*

(MATT *and* DEENA *appear inside the abandoned house.)*

DEENA. JUNIPER!

*(Lights shift as the women disappear into the darkness
and the music fades away with them.)*

(DEENA *rushes to* JUNIPER *and picks her up.)*

MATT. I didn't mean to – I'm sorry. We weren't doing anything, really she just started to – I freaked out, I didn't
know what to do….Is she gonna be alright?

(DEENA *carries her back into the house as* MATT *watches
from a distance and is gone. Once inside the house
DEENA places* JUNIPER *into her bed and watches her
until she wakes up.)*

DEENA. How do you feel?

(She sits up slowly.)

JUNIPER. It hurts.

DEENA. The cramping from your period. It may be like that
sometimes.
Junie? I like him. This Matt. He seems nice. But – I'd
be lying if I said that the two of you can – I know your
curious about sex and – It will be difficult for you to be
physical with Matt and not feel –

JUNIPER. I know. At first it felt *nice*. Then it felt like a bunch
of needles sticking me in one place.
And then I felt nothing.

(beat)

You never told me before. How old was I –

DEENA. Between the age of two and three. We've never known the exact date.

(**JUNIPER** *takes this in.*)

Do you *remember*?

JUNIPER. There were three women. One of them was my mother. I remember her eyes.

I just – Did she love me –

DEENA. Yes…She did.

When you were born you were loved *so much* – that a whole community got together and celebrated *your* life. They marched through the streets and they sang till their voices were gone. And then your mother took you in her arms and did what she believed in.

One day when we've found a way to help your body heal – a man you love very much is going to touch you. And you're going to feel it. Only it's not going to feel like needles. It's going to feel like you're soaking in a warm bath…only the water is *him*. And you're going to feel it from the bottom of you feet to the tip of your ears. You will, Juniper. You'll feel it.

(*A moment.*)

I'm sorry I've waited so long to talk about it.

(**JUNIPER** *lies in her mother's lap. She clings to her.* **DEENA** *caresses her for the first time.*)

DEENA. June bug.

(*She tries to remember.*)

DEENA. Juna ba – la - la long cuckoo
Juna ba – la – la long tweh tweh
Juna ba - la - la long cuckoo
Juna ba – la - la long tweh tweh

Fana - galo, Fana - galay
All the boys from Zulu land

Fana - galo, Fana - galay
All the boys from Zulu land

(**DEENA** *continues to caress her daughter as lights slowly fade to blackout.*)

OFF-OFF-BROADWAY
FESTIVAL PLAYS

TWELFTH SERIES
The Brannock Device   The Prettiest Girl in Lafayette County   Slivovitz
Two and Twenty

THIRTEENTH SERIES
Beached   A Grave Encounter   No Problem   Reservations for Two
Strawberry Preserves   What's a Girl to Do

FOURTEENTH SERIES
A Blind Date with Mary   Bums   Civilization and Its Malcontents   Do Over
Tradition 1A

FIFTEENTH SERIES
The Adventures of Captain Neato-Man   A Chance Meeting Chateau Rene
Does This Woman Have a Name?   For Anne   The Heartbreak Tour
The Pledge

SIXTEENTH SERIES
As Angels Watch   Autumn Leaves   Goods   King of the Pekinese Yellowtail
Uranium   Way Deep   The Whole Truth   The Winning Number

SEVENTEENTH SERIES
Correct Address   Cowboys, Indians and Waitresses   Homebound   The Road
to Nineveh   Your Life Is a Feature Film

EIGHTEENTH SERIES
How Many to Tango?   Just Thinking   Last Exit Before Toll   Pasquini the
Magnificent   Peace in Our Time   The Power and the Glory
Something Rotten in Denmark   Visiting Oliver

NINETEENTH SERIES
Awkward Silence   Cherry Blend with Vanilla   Family Names   Highwire
Nothing in Common   Pizza: A Love Story   The Spelling Bee

TWENTIETH SERIES
Pavane   The Art of Dating   Snow Stars   Life Comes to the Old Maid   The
Appointment   A Winter Reunion

TWENTY-FIRST SERIES
Whoppers   Dolorosa Sanchez   At Land's End   In with Alma
With or Without You   Murmurs   Ballycastle

SAMUELFRENCH.COM

OFF-OFF-BROADWAY
FESTIVAL PLAYS

TWENTY-SECOND SERIES
Brothers   This Is How It Is   Because I Wanted to Say   Tremulous   The Last
Dance   For Tiger Lilies Out of Season   The Most Perfect Day

TWENTY-THIRD SERIES
The Way to Miami   Harriet Tubman Visits a Therapist   Meridan, Mississippi
Studio Portrait   It's Okay, Honey   Francis Brick Needs No Introduction

TWENTY-FOURTH SERIES
The Last Cigarette   Flight of Fancy   Physical Therapy   Nothing in the World Like It
The Price You Pay   Pearls Ophelia   A Significant Betrayal

TWENTY-FIFTH SERIES
Strawberry Fields   Sin Inch Adjustable   Evening Education   Hot Rot
A Pink Cadillac Nightmare   East of the Sun and West of the Moon

TWENTY-SIXTH SERIES
Tickets, Please!   Someplace Warm   The Test   A Closer Look
A Peace Replaced   Three Tables

TWENTY-SEVENTH SERIES
Born to Be Blue   The Parrot   Flights   A Doctor's Visit
Three Questions   The Devil's Parole

TWENTY-EIGHTH SERIES
Along for the Ride   A Low-Lying Fog   Blueberry Waltz   The Ferry
Leaving Tangier   Quick & Dirty (A Subway Fantasy)

TWENTY-NINTH SERIES
All in Little Pieces   The Casseroles of Far Rockaway   Feet of Clay
The King and the Condemned   My Wife's Coat   The Theodore Roosevelt Rotunda

THIRTIETH SERIES
Defacing Michael Jackson   The Ex   Kerry and Angie   Outside the Box
Picture Perfect   The Sweet Room

THIRTY-FIRST SERIES
Le Supermarché   Libretto   Play #3   Sick   Pischer   Relationtrip

THIRTY-SECOND SERIES
Opening   Circuit Breakers   Bright. Apple. Crush
The Roosevelt Cousins, Thoroughly Sauced   Every Man   The Good Book

SAMUELFRENCH.COM

OTHER TITLES AVAILABLE FROM SAMUEL FRENCH

THE OFFICE PLAYS
Two full length plays by Adam Bock

THE RECEPTIONIST
Comedy / 2m., 2f. Interior

At the start of a typical day in the Northeast Office, Beverly deals effortlessly with ringing phones and her colleague's romantic troubles. But the appearance of a charming rep from the Central Office disrupts the friendly routine. And as the true nature of the company's business becomes apparent, The Receptionist raises disquieting, provocative questions about the consequences of complicity with evil.

"...Mr. Bock's poisoned Post-it note of a play." - *New York Times*

"Bock's intense initial focus on the routine goes to the heart of *The Receptionist's* pointed, painfully timely allegory... elliptical, provocative play..."
- *Time Out New York*

THE THUGS
Comedy / 2m, 6f / Interior

The Obie Award winning dark comedy about work, thunder and the mysterious things that are happening on the 9th floor of a big law firm. When a group of temps try to discover the secrets that lurk in the hidden crevices of their workplace, they realize they would rather believe in gossip and rumors than face dangerous realities.

"Bock starts you off giggling, but leaves you with a chill."
- *Time Out New York*

"... a delightfully paranoid little nightmare that is both more chillingly realistic and pointedly absurd than anything John Grisham ever dreamed up."
- *New York Times*

SAMUELFRENCH.COM